ISSUES

The Muslim Woman
SHOULD CONCERN HERSELF WITH

By Ash-Shaykh 'Abdullah bin Jaar Allah bin Ibraaheem al-Jaar Allah

قَضَايَا تَهمُّ المَرْأَةُ

Issues the Muslim Woman Should Concern Herself With

ISBN: 978-1-4507-6560-2

First Edition: Rabi II 1432 A.H. / March 2011 C.E.

Cover Design: **Typesetting:**
Usul Design   Proof 2 Print
E-mail: **Email:**
info@usuldesign.com   proof2print@gmail.com

Publisher's Information: Authentic Statements Publishing
P.O.Box 15536   **Store:**
Philadelphia, Pa. 19131 5312 Market St.
215.382-3382   Phila Pa 19139
215.382.3782-Fax

Website: authenticstatements.com
E-mail: info@authenticstatements.com

Please visit our website for upcoming publications, audio/Dvd online catalog, and info on events and seminars, insha Allah.

2

Contents

قَضَايَا تَهمُ المَرْأَةُ

Issues the Muslim Woman Should Concern Herself With

Biography of Shaykh 'Abdullah bin Jaar Allah[1] –may Allah have mercy on him

He is *ash-Shaykh* 'Abdullah bin Jaar Allah bin Ibraaheem Aali Jaar Allah. His lineage is traced back to the *Nawaasir* tribe of the *Banoo Tameem*. He was born in *al-Mudhnib* in the region of *al-Qaseem*. He had a righteous upbringing and from his youth he studied writing and memorized the Quran with his father. He travelled to *ar-Riyaadh* in the year 1368 A.H. and again in 1374 A.H. He took knowledge from *ash-Shaykh* Muhmamd bin Ibraaheem Aali ash-Shaykh. In the year 1375 A.H. he attended the *Imaam-ad-Da'wah* Institute where he studied under a number of scholars, from them *ash-Shaykh* Ismaa'eel bin Muhammad al-Ansaaree, as well as others.

He graduated from this institute in 1379 A.H. and then he attended the College of *ash-Shar'eeah* (Islamic Law) in *ar-Riyaadh* where he graduated in 1384 A.H. He was appointed as a teacher by the Ministry of Education. He taught in the middle schools in *Haail*

---

[1] Source: http://www.alukah.net/Web/jarallah/CV/

5

---

and *Buraydah* in 1386 A.H. Then he moved to *ar-Riyaadh* for the same type of work. He then attended the Advanced Institute for Islamic Judges where he obtained his Masters in *al-Fiqh al-Muqaarin* (Comparative Islamic Jurisprudence) in the year 1399 A.H. In the year 1403 A.H. he moved to teach in the high schools and remained there until he had to retire because of his failing health.

He was one who constantly engaged in all acts of worship such as prayer, fasting, and supplications. He is mentioned with loving knowledge, with reviewing it and studying with others. He spent his time in that which was beneficial. He was humble and always smiling. He was patient, generous, and compassionate for the poor and the needy. He exerted all of his efforts, work time, free time, and wealth in the path of calling to Allah, advising and counseling, with money and by the pen. He died in Makkah al-Mukarramah in the spring of the 20th of Ramadan.

It has been mentioned that he authored more than one hundred and fifty treatises, mostly short and beneficial, that treated the important issues that the general people were in need of knowing. Many have been printed and distributed with wide acceptance, and many have benefited from them.

قَضَايَا تَهُمُّ المَرْأَةُ

Issues the Muslim Woman Should Concern Herself With

Introduction

All praise is for Allah, Lord of all the worlds. I bear witness that there is nothing worthy of worship except for Allah alone, He has no partner. And I bear witness that Muhammad is His servant and His messenger, peace be upon him, his family, and all of his companions. To proceed:

I decided to select individual sections from my book *ath-Thammaar al-Yaani'ah min al-Kalimaat al-Jaami'ah* (The Ripe Fruits taken from the Comprehensive Words)[2], issues concerning the Muslim woman towards her Lord, her religion, her temporal life, and her hereafter by encouraging knowledge of the following: Marriage and explaining its benefits, warning from extravagant dowries and explaining its harms, mentioning the connections harbored between the spouses from the Islamic viewpoint, the permissibility of polygyny in Islam, the necessity of Muslim women observing the proper Islamic head covering, an explanation of the rulings for the wife

---

[2] **T.N:** This is a larger book of about 550 pages that includes important modern issues affecting Muslims today, such as dealing with usury, seeking knowledge, working in banks that deal with usury, smoking, homosexuality, and much more.

قَضَايَا تَهمُّ المَرْأةُ

Issues the Muslim Woman Should Concern Herself With

---

mourning the loss of her husband, the dangers of intermingling between men and women who are not related to one another, the descriptions of the women of paradise and the descriptions of the women of the hellfire and encouragement to save the souls and family from it, an explanation of the ruling surrounding shaking hands with non-relative women, an explanation on the rulings of menstruation, continuous vaginal bleeding , and post-natal bleeding, what has been mentioned concerning charity tax on jewelry, an explanation on the prohibition of women displaying their beauty and intermingling with men and the command to observe the proper head covering around them, women have half of the men in some of the Islamic rulings, and evaluating equality between a woman and man in the light of Islam.

I have singled out these issues to be easily referenced, (to provide a) light carrying (booklet), and derived from the speech of Allah, Most High, and the speech of His messenger, peace be upon him, in addition to the scholars who verified (the correct from the false).

I ask Allah, Most High to benefit whoever reads, hears, or prints this. And I ask Him to make it

---

sincerely for His generous face. May the causes of victory be the tranquility of paradise. He is sufficient for us and the best one entrusted. There is no power or strength except by Allah, the Lofty, the Great. And may peace and blessings be upon our Prophet Muhammad, his family, and all of his companions.

Chapter One: Marriage and its benefits

All praise is for Allah, Lord of the worlds. I bear witness that there is nothing worthy of worship except for Allah alone, He has no partner. I bear witness that Muhammad is His servant and His messenger, may peace and blessings be upon his family and companions. May many complete salutations of peace be sent upon the Prophet until the Day of Judgment. To proceed:

Allah has legislated marriage as an exalted decree with excellent objectives and important benefits. He has commanded its end results to be easily obtained since it is a sound path to conception and building righteous offspring upon the earth.

Allah the Most High says:

﴿ فَٱنكِحُواْ مَا طَابَ لَكُم مِّنَ ٱلنِّسَآءِ مَثْنَىٰ وَثُلَٰثَ وَرُبَٰعَ ۖ فَإِنْ خِفْتُمْ أَلَّا تَعْدِلُواْ فَوَٰحِدَةً أَوْ مَا مَلَكَتْ أَيْمَٰنُكُمْ ۚ ﴿٣﴾ ﴾

قَضَايَا تَهُمُّ المَرْأَةُ

Issues the Muslim Woman Should Concern Herself With

_____

{Then marry (other) women of your choice, two or three, or four; but if you fear that you shall not be able to deal justly (with them), then only one or (the slaves) that your right hands possess.}[3]

And the Most High says:

$$﴿ وَمِنْ ءَايَٰتِهِۦٓ أَنْ خَلَقَ لَكُم مِّنْ أَنفُسِكُمْ أَزْوَٰجًا لِّتَسْكُنُوٓا۟ إِلَيْهَا وَجَعَلَ بَيْنَكُم مَّوَدَّةً وَرَحْمَةً ۚ إِنَّ فِى ذَٰلِكَ لَآيَٰتٍ لِّقَوْمٍ يَتَفَكَّرُونَ ۩ ﴾$$

{And among His Signs is this, that He created for you wives from among yourselves, that you may find repose in them, and He has put between you affection and mercy. Verily, in that are indeed signs for a people who reflect.}[4]

_____

[3] An-Nisaa'a: 3
[4] Ar-Room: 21

قَضَايَا تَهُمُّ المَرْأَةُ

Issues the Muslim Woman Should Concern Herself With

And the Most High says:

﴿ وَأَنكِحُوا۟ ٱلْأَيَـٰمَىٰ مِنكُمْ وَٱلصَّـٰلِحِينَ مِنْ عِبَادِكُمْ وَإِمَآئِكُمْ ۚ إِن يَكُونُوا۟ فُقَرَآءَ يُغْنِهِمُ ٱللَّهُ مِن فَضْلِهِۦ ۗ وَٱللَّهُ وَٰسِعٌ عَلِيمٌ ۝ ﴾

{And marry those among you who are single (i.e. a man who has no wife and the woman who has no husband) and (also marry) the Sâlihûn (pious, fit and capable ones) of your (male) slaves and maid-servants (female slaves). If they be poor, Allâh will enrich them out of His Bounty. And Allâh is All-Sufficient for His creatures' needs, All-Knowing (about the state of the people).}[5]

Aboo Bakr as-Sideeq (the Truthful), may Allah be pleased with him, said, "Obey Allah in whatever He commands you regarding marriage, He will grant you wealth that is promised for you."

----

[5] An-Noor: 32

The Arabic word الأيامى al-Ayaamaa is the plural of أيم Ayyim which are the men and women who have no spouse.

And the Prophet, peace be upon him, said:

يَا مَعْشَرَ الشَّبَابِ مَنِ اسْتَطَاعَ مِنْكُم الْبَاءَةَ فَلْيَتَزَوَّجْ فَإِنَّهُ أَغَضُّ لِلْبَصَرِ وَ أَحْصَنُ لِلْفَرْجِ وَ مَنْ لَمْ يَسْتَطِعْ فَعَلَيْهِ بِالصَّوْمِ فَإِنَّهُ لَهُ وَجَاءٌ

(O assembly of young men, whoever amongst you has al-Baa'ah should marry as it causes one to lower his gaze and is foremost in protecting the private parts. But whoever from amongst you cannot (marry), then he should fast as it will be a Wajaa'a for him.)[6]

The meaning of the Arabic word الباءة al-Baa'ah means provisions for marriage. The word الوجاء al-Wajaa'a means a protection from sexual desire.

The Prophet, peace be upon him, rejected the one who abstained from marriage and other permissible acts when he said:

---

[6] Related by al-Bukhaaree, Muslim, and others.

14

لِكِنِّي أَصُومُ وَ أُفْطِرُ وَ أُصَلِّي وَ أَنَامُ وَ أَتَزَوَّجُ النِّسَاءَ فَمَنْ رَغِبَ عَنْ
سُنَّتِي فَلَيْسَ مِنِّي

(...But I fast and I break my fast. I sleep and I marry women. Whoever abstains from my *Sunnah* is not from me.)

And he, peace be upon him said:

الدُّنْيَا مَتَاعٌ وَ خَيْرُ مَتَاعِهَا المَرْأَةُ الصَّالِحَةُ

(The temporal world is pleasure. The best of those things that are pleasurable are the righteous wife.)[7]

And it has been narrated by Anas, may Allah be pleased with him, that the Messenger of Allah, peace be upon him said:

مَنْ رَزَقَهُ اللَّهُ امْرَأَةً صَالِحَةً فَقَدْ أَعَانَهُ عَلَى شَطْرِ دِينِهِ فَلْيَتَّقِ اللَّهَ فِي
الشَّطْرِ البَاقِي

(Whoever Allah provides with a righteous wife, it will help him with half of his religion, so fear Allah regarding the other half.)[8]

---

[7] It is agreed upon by al-Bukhaaree and Muslim.
[8] Related by Muslim.

And in another narrative, he, peace be upon him, said:

إِذَا تَزَوَّجَ الْعَبْدُ فَقَدِ اسْتَكْمَلَ نِصْفَ الدِّيْن فَلْيَتَّقِ اللَّهَ فِي النِّصْفِ الْبَاقِي

(When the servant marries then he completes half of his religion, so fear Allah in regards to the other half.)[9]

And from Aboo Hurayrah, may Allah be pleased with him, who said that the Messenger of Allah, peace be upon him, said:

ثَلَاثَة حَقٌّ عَلَى اللَّهِ عَونهم: الْمُجَاهِد فِي سَبِيْلِ اللَّهِ وَ الْمَكَاتب يُرِيْدُ الأَدَاءَ وَ النِّكَاح يُرِيْدُ العفَاف

(There are three people whom Allah has obligated Himself the right to assistance; the one who strives in the path of Allah, the servant who desires to pay off his debt, and the person who marries desiring modesty.)[10]

---

[9] Related by at-Tabaraanee in al-Awsaat, al-Haakim who said that the chain of transmission is authentic, and al-Bayhaqee.

[10] Related by at-Tirmidhee, who said that the narration is good and authentic, Ibn Hibbaan in his *Saheeh*, and al-Haakim, who said it was authentic based on the condition of Muslim.

قَضَايَا تَـهمُّ المَرْأةُ

Issues the Muslim Woman Should Concern Herself With

Ibn Katheer said, "It is well known that from Allah's nobility and generousness is that He provides what is sufficient for her and for him."

It was related by Aboo Hurayrah, may Allah be pleased with him, that the Messenger of Allah, peace be upon him, said:

تُنْكَحُ المَرْأةُ لِأرْبَع : لِمَالِهَا وَ لِحَسَبِهَا وَ لِجَمَالِهَا وَ لِدِيْنِهَا فاظْفَرْ بذَاتِ الدِّيْنِ تَرِبَتْ يَدَاكَ

(The woman is married for four reasons; for her wealth, her lineage, her beauty, and for her religion, so choose the one possessing religion, may your hand be covered in dust.)[11]

And Sa'eed bin Jubayr said, "Ibn 'Abbaas said to me, 'Did you marry?' to which I said, "no". He replied, 'Get married for indeed it is the best thing for this *Ummah*, the best part of it is women.'"[12]

And the Prophet, peace be upon him, said:

---

[11] Related by al-Bukhaaree, Muslim, and others.
[12] Related by Ahmad and al-Bukhaaree.

أرْبَع مَنْ أُعْطِيهُنَّ فَقَدْ أُعْطِيَ خَيْرُ الدُّنْيَا وَ الآخِرَة قلْبًا شَاكِرًا وَ لِسَانًا
ذَاكِرًا وَ بَدَنًا عَلَى البَلاء صَابِرًا وَ زَوْجَة لاَ تَبْغِيهِ حوبًّا فِي نَفْسِهَا وَ
مَالِهِ

(There are four things that are the best things of this life and the hereafter that can be given; a thankful heart, a tongue that constantly (remembers Allah), a person patient with affliction, and a wife that does not commit sin against herself and her husband's property.)[13]

Ibn Mas'ood said, "If only ten days of my life span remained and I knew I was going to die the last day, and I only had the length of the marriage contract then I would marry out of fear of seduction."

And Imam Ahmad said, "Celibacy is not a part of Islam. Whoever calls on you not to get married then he is not calling you to Islam. If a person marries then the religion is completed."

And *Shaykh-ul-Islam* Ibn Taymiyyah said in his book *al-Ikhteeyaaraat*, "Rejecting family and children is not from what Allah and His messenger loves. It is not

---

[13] Related by at-Tabaraanee with a good chain of transmission.

---

from the religion of the Prophets. Allah Most High says:

﴿ وَلَقَدْ أَرْسَلْنَا رُسُلاً مِّن قَبْلِكَ وَجَعَلْنَا لَهُمْ

أَزْوَاجًا وَذُرِّيَّةً ۞ ﴾

{And indeed We sent Messengers before you (O Muhammad (peace be upon him)) and made for them wives and offspring.}[14]

My Muslim brother, marriage is cultivated soil for offspring, a place of rest for the soul, a pleasure of life, a comforter of the heart, a fortress for the body parts, just as it is a blessing, relaxation, a *Sunnah*, a cover, protection, a cause to obtain righteous offspring that will benefit mankind in this life and after death. Marriage in Islam is a binding arrangement, a sacred covenant, a social obligation, a spiritual place and path to love and mercy between men and women. It removes the most instinctive confusions embedded within the heart and mind. The soul does not rest or is filled with tranquility

---

[14] Ar-Ra'd: 38

19

_____

without it, just as it is an act of worship that a person completes half of his religion. He will encounter his Lord upon the best condition of chastity and purity. Fear Allah youth of Islam! Lower your gaze from looking at the prohibited and protect your private parts with the good things that are permissible. Obey your Lord in what He has commanded you concerning marriage, He will grant you wealth that is promised for you. Beware of abstaining from marriage fearing to take on its responsibilities, the issue is dependent on Allah Most High in granting happiness after difficulty and hardship, ease only comes after difficulty. You read what was previously mentioned concerning the promise of the Most High for the one who marries; wealth, assistance, and provision when one fears Allah Most High and obeys Him and relies on Him in all of one's affairs:

﴿ وَمَن يَتَّقِ ٱللَّهَ تَجْعَل لَّهُ مَخْرَجًا ۝ وَيَرْزُقْهُ مِنْ حَيْثُ لَا يَحْتَسِبُ ۝ ﴾

{And whosoever fears Allâh and keeps his duty to Him, He will make a way for him to get out (from

----

every difficulty). And He will provide him from (sources) he never could imagine.}[15]

And He says:

﴿ وَمَن يَتَّقِ ٱللَّهَ يَجْعَل لَّهُۥ مِنْ أَمْرِهِۦ يُسْرًا ۝ ﴾

{And whosoever fears Allâh and keeps his duty to Him, He will make his matter easy for him.}[16]

---

[15] At-Talaaq: 2-3
[16] At-Talaaq: 4

Chapter Two: From the Many Benefits of getting Married

Marriage has benefits that are religious, secular, social, and health-based. We will mention some:

One – Obedience to the command of Allah and His messenger, which results in the servant's happiness, in this life and in the hereafter.

Two – Following the ways of the Messengers who commanded us to follow them and emulate them.

Three – Fulfilling the objective of joy for the soul and happiness of the heart.

Four – Protection of the private parts, defense of honor, lowering of the eyesight, and distancing one's self from seduction and lust.

Five – Increasing the Islamic nation as numbers strengthen it and causes the other nations to respect it. (In addition), It will suffice itself from (relying on) others if its strength is used in implementing the purified legislation.

Six - The fulfillment of the Prophet's pride, peace be upon him, for his nation on the Day of Judgment.

Seven - Connecting the families and strengthening the bonds of love between families and emphasizing a social connection. Indeed a tightly-knit society is a happy and strong society.

Eight - Marriage is a cause for provisions and wealth to increase as has proceeded in the statement of the Most High: {If they are poor, Allah will increase them from His favor.} And the statement of the Prophet, peace be upon him: (There are three people whom Allah has obligated Himself the right to assistance...) and he mentioned from them: (the person who marries desiring modesty).

Nine - The continuation of the human species by way of procreation which results from being married, and causes joy through the occurrence of children.

Ten - The need of both of the spouses for one another; mentally, physically, and spiritually.

Eleven - (The institute of marriage) follows the natural and deep-rooted desire embedded within

---

men and women which Allah placed within them to perfect human life.

Twelve - (Marriage is) cooperation of both spouses in raising their children, building a family, and protecting it.

Thirteen - Classifying the bond between man and woman on the basis of mutually observing each other's rights and upon cooperation that promotes love, mercy, companionship, respect, and appreciation.

Fourteen - Obtaining the great repayment and immense reward for establishing the rights of the wife and children by spending on them. The Prophet, peace be upon him, said: (In some of you is charity.) The companions said, "O Messenger of Allah, one of us is overcome with sexual desire, there is a reward for fulfilling it?" He said: (Don't you see if one engaged in impermissible sex it would be a sin? Likewise when one engages in the permissible act of sex then he is rewarded.)[17]

---

[17] Related by Muslim.

And he said, peace be upon him: (Indeed you will never spend anything seeking from it the reward of Allah except that you are rewarded for it, even for the inheritance that you leave for your wife.)[18]

Fifteen – Marriage completes the religion, purifies the soul and body, and protects one's honor.

Sixteen – The supplication of the righteous child for his parents as the Prophet, peace be upon him said:

إِذَا مَاتَ ابْنُ آدَم انْقَطَعَ عَمَلُهُ إِلاَّ مِنْ ثَلاثٍ : صَدَقَةٌ جَارِيَةٌ أَوْ عِلْمٌ يَنْتَفِعُ بِهِ أَوْ وَلَدٌ صَالِحٌ يَدْعُو لَهُ

(When one of the children of Adam dies, all of his good deeds are cut off except for three; permanent charity (such as a well, donated library, etc.), Knowledge that was left to be benefited from or a righteous child that supplicates for him.)[19]

Seventeen – Protection from the devil, defense against the harms of lust, and abstaining from sex out of wedlock.

---

[18] Agreed upon by al-Bukhaaree and Muslim.
[19] Related by Muslim.

Eighteen – Preserving one's lineage and the rights of inheritance.

Nineteen – (From the benefits of marriage is) the rejuvenation of the soul and promoting companionship by engaging in marital dialogue, intimacy, looking at the permissible, and flirting and playing around with one another which eases the heart and strengthens one's worship.

Twenty – What has come from the editorial of the United Nations that married couples live longer than those who are not married; based on that it is stated that marriage benefits the health of the man and woman together.

Twenty One – Struggling with the soul and its activeness in guardianship, authority, and the establishment of the rights of the family and children in bearing responsibility for them while observing patience and getting the rewards of what it is arranged.

Twenty Two – Islam has made marriage an act of worship because by it the soul is protected from the

---

evils of tribulations and from the harmful look as well as from falling into corruption.

Twenty Three – The conservation of every individual and society from moral disintegration as well as preservation from spiritual and physical sicknesses. Whoever can get married then he should rush into fulfilling these benefits and numerous advantages that marriage is set up upon. And whoever cannot then he should be patient and fear Allah Most High and be modest of what Allah has prohibited, and lower his gaze and protect his private parts. He should protect himself with fasting until Allah the Most High blesses him with the bounty of affluence.

The Most High says:

$$\text{﴿ وَلْيَسْتَعْفِفِ ٱلَّذِينَ لَا يَجِدُونَ نِكَاحًا حَتَّىٰ يُغْنِيَهُمُ ٱللَّهُ مِن فَضْلِهِۦ ۗ ﴿٣٣﴾ ﴾}$$

قَضَايَا تَهُمُّ الْمَرْأَةُ
Issues the Muslim Woman Should Concern Herself With

{And let those who find not the financial means for marriage keep themselves chaste, until Allâh enriches them of His Bounty.}[20]

And the previous narration where the Prophet, peace be upon him, said:

يَا مَعْشَرَ الشَّبَابِ مَنِ اسْتَطَاعَ مِنْكُمُ الْبَاءَةَ فَلْيَتَزَوَّجْ فَإِنَّهُ أَغَضُ لِلْبَصَرِ
وَ أَحْصَنُ لِلْفَرْجِ وَ مَنْ لَمْ يَسْتَطِعْ فَعَلَيْهِ بِالصَّوْمِ فَإِنَّهُ لَهُ وَجَاءٌ

(O assembly of young men, whoever amongst you has the financial means should marry as it causes one to lower his gaze and is foremost in protecting the private parts. But whoever from amongst you cannot (marry), then he should fast as it will be a protection for him.)

And with Allah is all success. May the peace and blessings of Allah be upon his family and companions.

---

[20] An-Noor: 3

28

Chapter Three: Extravagant Dowries and their Harms

There is no doubt that marriage is a necessity from the many necessities of life; when it is accomplished many benefits, both religious and secular, are obtained. It causes a bond between people. It is a means of obtaining love and mutual compassion for one another. The husband lives within his wife and the wife within her husband. The Most High says:

﴿ وَمِنْ ءَايَٰتِهِۦٓ أَنْ خَلَقَ لَكُم مِّنْ أَنفُسِكُمْ أَزْوَٰجًا لِّتَسْكُنُوٓاْ إِلَيْهَا وَجَعَلَ بَيْنَكُم مَّوَدَّةً وَرَحْمَةً إِنَّ فِى ذَٰلِكَ لَأٓيَٰتٍ لِّقَوْمٍ يَتَفَكَّرُونَ ۞ ﴾

{And among His Signs is this, that He created for you wives from among yourselves, that you may find repose in them, and He has put between you affection and mercy. Verily, in that are indeed signs for a people who reflect.}[21]

---

[21] Ar-Room: 21

29

By marrying the propagation of offspring occurs, which is a response to the Prophet's call, peace be upon him, to marry, as it occurs in the prophetic narration that he said:

تَزَوَّجُوا الْوَلُودَ الْوَدُودَ فَإِنِّي مُكَاثِرٌ بِكُم الْأُمَم

(Marry the fertile and loving, for indeed I will be proud of your great number before the other nations on the Day of Judgment.)[22]

Marriage is more conducive in lowering the gaze, protecting the private parts, and in observing modesty. We hold married life to be much better than bachelorhood. The married person, his soul is tranquil and his livelihood is comfortable. The causes of comfort, gentleness, and humbleness will increase and by that the issues of his religion and secular life are sanctified, as it is related in the prophetic narration:

إِذَا تَزَوَّجَ الْعَبْدُ فَقَدِ اسْتَكْمَلَ نِصْفَ الدِّيْن فَلْيَتَّقَ اللَّهَ فِي النِّصْفِ الْبَاقِي

---

[22] Related by Aboo Daawud and an-Nisaa'ee.

(When the servant marries then he completes half of his religion, so fear Allah in regards to the other half.)[23]

This is especially true if one is granted a righteous and obedient wife, one who watches over what Allah has ordered to be watched over. When he looks at her she pleases him. If he tells her to do something she obeys him. If he is absent she protects her modesty and his property. Many Quranic verses and prophetic narrations have been revealed concerning the issue of marriage and the encouragement to do so. From them is the statement of Allah Most High:

﴿ فَٱنكِحُواْ مَا طَابَ لَكُم مِّنَ ٱلنِّسَآءِ مَثۡنَىٰ وَثُلَٰثَ وَرُبَٰعَ ۖ ۝ ﴾

{Then marry (other) women of your choice, two or three, or four.}[24]

And the Most High says:

---

[23] Related by at-Tabaraanee in al-Awsaat, al-Haakim who said that the chain of transmission is authentic, and al-Bayhaqee.

[24] An-Nisaa'a: 3

﴿ وَأَنكِحُواْ ٱلْأَيَـٰمَىٰ مِنكُمْ وَٱلصَّـٰلِحِينَ مِنْ عِبَادِكُمْ
وَإِمَآئِكُمْ ۚ إِن يَكُونُواْ فُقَرَآءَ يُغْنِهِمُ ٱللَّهُ مِن فَضْلِهِۦ ۗ وَٱللَّهُ
وَٰسِعٌ عَلِيمٌ ۝ ﴾

{And marry those among you who are single (i.e. a man who has no wife and the woman who has no husband) and (also marry) the Sâlihûn (pious, fit and capable ones) of your (male) slaves and maid-servants (female slaves). If they be poor, Allâh will enrich them out of His Bounty. And Allâh is All-Sufficient for His creatures' needs, All-Knowing (about the state of the people).}[25]

The *Ayaamaa* الأيامى is plural of أيم *Ayyim* which are the men and women who have not married. This verse encourages marriage and promises the person who marries with affluence after having had nothing. Aboo Bakr as-Sideeq (the Truthful), may Allah be pleased with him, said, "Obey Allah in whatever He commands you regarding marriage, He will grant you wealth that is promised for you."

---

[25] An-Noor: 32

Ibn Mas'ood, may Allah be pleased with him said, "Seek wealth in order to get married."

﴿ إِن يَكُونُوا فُقَرَاءَ يُغْنِهِمُ اللَّهُ مِن فَضْلِهِ ۗ

وَاللّٰه وَاسِعٌ عَلِيمٌ ۝ ﴾

{...If they be poor, Allâh will enrich them out of His Bounty. And Allâh is All-Sufficient for His creatures' needs, All-Knowing (about the state of the people).}[26]

And in the prophetic narration:

ثَلَاثَةٌ حَقٌّ عَلَى اللهِ عَوْنهم : المُتَزَوِّج يُرِيْدُ العفَافَ وَ المُكَاتبُ يُرِيْدُ الأَدَاءَ وَ الغَازي فِي سَبِيْلِ اللهِ

(There are three people whom Allah has obligated Himself the right to assistance; the person who marries desiring modesty, the servant who desires to pay off his debt, and the one who strives in the path of Allah.)[27]

---

[26] An-Noor: 32
[27] Related by Ahmad, at-Tirmidhee, an-Nisaa'ee, and Ibn Maajah.

33

Ibn Katheer said, "It is well known that from Allah's nobility and generousness is that He provides what is sufficient for her and for him."

Therefore it is befitting for one who is able to get married to marry in obedience to the command of Allah and His Messenger and to observe modesty towards himself and his wife. Avoiding marriage results in numerous harms, from them; the impermissible look, which is a poisonous arrow utilized from the arrows of *Iblees*, it is a path to adultery. (And from them) are illnesses that hinder the person because of choosing not to marry. Unfortunately we see many young men adverse to the legislated manners of marriage, fleeing from its responsibilities. In that is a great danger for them and their nation. The Messenger of Allah, peace be upon him, the one who was compassionate and merciful to his *Ummah* (the Islamic nation) said:

يَا مَعْشَرَ الشَّبَابِ مَنِ اسْتَطَاعَ مِنْكُم البَاءَةَ فَلْيَتَزَوَّجْ فَإِنَّهُ أَغَضُّ لِلْبَصَرِ
وَ أَحْصَنُ لِلْفَرْجِ وَ مَنْ لَمْ يَسْتَطِعْ فَعَلَيْهِ بِالصَّوْمِ فَإِنَّهُ لَهُ وَجَاء

(O assembly of young men, whoever amongst you has the financial means should marry as it causes one to lower his gaze and is foremost in protecting the

----

private parts. But whoever from amongst you cannot (marry), then he should fast as it will be a protection for him.)

The financial means mentioned here are the provisions used for marriage and the burdens that come with it. This narration encourages marriage since it protects the private parts and lowers the gaze. It is related by Anas bin Maalik, may Allah be pleased with him, who said that the Prophet, peace be upon him, praised Allah and praised His qualities, then he said:

لكِنِّي أَصُومُ وَ أَفْطِرُ وَ أُصَلِّي وَ أَنَامُ وَ أَتَزَوَّجُ النِّسَاءَ فَمَنْ رَغِبَ عَنْ سُنَّتِي فَلَيْسَ مِنِّي

(...But I fast and I break my fast. I sleep and I marry women. Whoever abstains from my *Sunnah* is not from me.)[28]

----

[28] Agreed upon by al-Bukhaaree and Muslim.

قَضَايَا تَهمُّ المَرْأَةُ
Issues the Muslim Woman Should Concern Herself With

Many people today cannot get married because of extravagant marriage dowries and the high costs associated with the marriage ceremonies. It is a difficult problem harming society. Only Allah knows how many young men and women have been oppressed because of this. It has not been relayed from the Prophet, peace be upon him, or any of the companions or their students that they spent on extravagant dowries nor were they commanded to do so. It is narrated that the Prophet, peace be upon him, said:

إِذَا جَاءَكُمْ مَنْ تَرْضَوْنَ دِيْنَهُ وَ خُلُقَهُ فَأَنْكِحُوهُ إِلاَّ تَفْعَلُوا تَكُنْ فِتْنَة فِي الأَرْضِ وَ فَسَاد

(Whenever one comes to you whose practice of the religion and good manners please you then get him married if not there will be corruption and tribulations upon the earth.)[29]

And in a narrative of at-Tirmidhee:

إِذَا خَطَبَ إِلَيْكُمْ مَنْ تَرْضَوْنَ دِيْنَهُ وَ خُلُقَهُ فَزَوِّجُوهُ إِلاَّ تَفْعَلُوا تَكُنْ فِتْنَة فِي الأَرْضِ وَ فَسَاد عَرِيْض

----

[29] Related by at-Tirmidhee who said that it was a good narration, and Ibn Maajah and al-Haakim.

قَضَايَا تَهُمُّ المَرْأَةُ

Issues the Muslim Woman Should Concern Herself With

(When one comes to you asking for your women's hands in marriage and whose practice of the religion and good manners pleases you, then marry him to them, if not there will be tribulations and widespread corruption upon the earth.)

And he, peace be upon him, said:

إِنَّ أَعْظَمَ النِّكَاحِ بَرَكَةً أَيْسَرُهُ مَؤُنَةً

(The most blessed of marriages is the one with the least expenses.)[30]

The dowries of the wives and daughters of the Prophet, peace be upon him, was five hundred Dirham. He once married a woman to a poor man who had nothing to give except from what he had memorized from the Quran. He told him afterwards:

إِلْتَمِسْ وَ لَوْ خَاتِمًا مِنْ حَدِيدٍ فَلَمْ يَجِد شَيْئًا

(Seek a ring of steel if nothing else is available.)[31]

---

[30] It is related by Ahmad and al-Bayhaqee in *Shu'ab-il-Imaan*.
[31] Related by al-Bukhaaree and Muslim.

And he married 'Abdur-Rahman bin 'Awf, may Allah be pleased with him, to a woman for the weight of a date pit in gold.

Allah Most High says:

$$ ﴿ لَّقَدْ كَانَ لَكُمْ فِى رَسُولِ ٱللَّهِ أُسْوَةٌ حَسَنَةٌ لِّمَن كَانَ يَرْجُواْ ٱللَّهَ وَٱلْيَوْمَ ٱلْأَخِرَ وَذَكَرَ ٱللَّهَ كَثِيرًا ۝ ﴾ $$

{Indeed in the Messenger of Allâh (Muhammad (peace be upon him)) you have a good example to follow for him who hopes for (the Meeting with) Allâh and the Last Day, and remembers Allâh much.}[32]

It is not wise or beneficial to be extravagant with the dowries and to waste money on the wedding ceremonies, or for the guardians to request excessive amounts of wealth from the groom which a poor person cannot fulfill. This causes the teenage males and females to be excluded (from the institution of marriage) and (to fall into) not being married.

---

[32] Al-Ahzaab: 21

Extravagance in dowries makes the wife out to be some type of commodity that is bought and sold because it violates manhood and contradicts customs and good manners.

It is befitting for whoever cannot marry to fast and be chaste until Allah Most High blesses him from His bounty as the Most High says:

$$\left\{ \text{وَلْيَسْتَعْفِفِ الَّذِينَ لَا يَجِدُونَ نِكَاحًا حَتَّىٰ يُغْنِيَهُمُ اللَّهُ مِن فَضْلِهِ ۗ ﴿٣٣﴾} \right\}$$

{And let those who find not the financial means for marriage keep themselves chaste, until Allâh enriches them of His Bounty.}[33]

And the Prophet, peace be upon him, said in the previous narration:

يَا مَعْشَرَ الشَّبَابِ مَنِ اسْتَطَاعَ مِنْكُمُ الْبَاءَةَ فَلْيَتَزَوَّجْ فَإِنَّهُ أَغَضُّ لِلْبَصَرِ وَ أَحْصَنُ لِلْفَرْجِ وَ مَنْ لَمْ يَسْتَطِعْ فَعَلَيْهِ بِالصَّوْمِ فَإِنَّهُ لَهُ وِجَاء

---

[33] An-Noor: 33

(O assembly of young men, whoever amongst you has the financial means should marry as it causes one to lower his gaze and is foremost in protecting the private parts. But whoever from amongst you cannot (marry), then he should fast as it will be a protection for him.)

It is a responsibility upon the guardians over the young men and women to make the dowries cheap and to facilitate the paths to marriage. The poor and their welfare should be taken into consideration, not greed and indulgence. Marrying the single Muslims and facilitating it fulfils social responsibilities and Islamic partnership. It spreads brotherhood, love, and cooperation amongst the Muslims who are like one body, like one strong structure, built one upon the other. May Allah grant all success of what He loves and is pleased with and may the peace and blessings of Allah be upon our Prophet Muhammad and upon his family and all of his companions.

Chapter Four: The Connection of the Spouses according to the Islamic View

All praise is for Allah, Lord of the worlds, and may peace and blessings be upon the noblest of the Prophets and Messengers, our Prophet and Imam, Muhammad, and upon his family and all of his companions. To proceed:

Islam has placed eminent boundaries concerning the rights of the husband and the wife. We will see how Islam made these rights harbor love and fulfillment. We will also mention some of the rights of the husband over the wife and the rights of the wife over the husband. We will begin with the rights of the husband over his wife:

One - Obedience of the wife to her husband based on what is good which is obedience dictated by the moral common interest between all partners. It isn't the obedience of the slave to his master, nor is it of one despised by one who subjugated the other. On the contrary, it is like obedience of a younger brother to his older brother. This is the obedience that Islam requires from the wife to her husband, and it is the

41

---

guardianship that the Quran refers to by its statement:

$$ \text{﴿ ٱلرِّجَالُ قَوَّٰمُونَ عَلَى ٱلنِّسَآءِ ﴾} $$

{Men are the protectors and maintainers of women.}[34]

Two - To be mindful of his feelings, keeping him from anything that may hurt him such as statements, actions or bad manners. And to take into account his financial circumstances and social status, not becoming annoyed by his work outside of the home as long as it's an honest living and he earns money from it. She shouldn't pressure him to buy things he isn't able to provide for her to the point that he will steal for it or become indebted. It was a habit of the women of the rightly-guided predecessors, may Allah be pleased with them, whether a wife or daughter of a man to say when he leaves the house:

اتَّقِ اللهَ وَ إِيَّاكَ وَ كَسْبَ الحَرَامِ فَإِنَّا نَصْبِرُ عَلَى الجُوعِ وَ الضَّرِّ وَ لَا نَصْبِرُ عَلَى النَّارِ

---

[34] An-Nisaa'a: 34

42

"Fear Allah and beware of forbidden earnings. Indeed we are patience with hunger and harm, but we will not show patience with the hellfire."

Three - For the wife to provide him with self-accommodation and contentment in the house by keeping herself and her house clean, and beautifying herself for him while providing what brings him closer to her and increases his love and longing for her. That is how a woman gains her husband's heart, not like one who meets her husband with kitchen clothes and unkempt hair looking disheveled and only beautifies herself when she goes out of the house or prepares for a visitor.

Four - Not to leave his house without his permission: Not to reveal her beauty to men she is allowed to marry. It is from the commandments of the Messenger of Allah, may the peace and blessings of Allah be upon him, that the wife is not to leave from her husband's house without his permission. If she did this, meaning left without her husband's permission, the angels curse her until she returns.[35]

---

[35] It was reported by at-Tabaraanee and al-Mundhiree pointed out its weakness.

43

Five - The wife should give him free time for himself and his thoughts. If he is one who spends his time in acts of worship she should allow him time to devote himself to wholeheartedly worshipping Allah in full submission. If he is one who is a scholar then she should allow him time to read, write, think or author. The pleasure that the worshipper finds in seclusion, or the scholar in his reading, and the writer in peacefulness is incomparable in life and the wife who does not feel this pleasure will not understand the meaning of it. She will see this as hatred, or of him being distant from her, so because of this she drives herself and her husband crazy.

As for the rights of the wife upon her husband then they are:

One – The husband must see his wife as a place of peace that was left for him to feel peaceful in. And (he must) complete her surroundings by giving her peace of mind along with a decent life coupled with happiness. The noble Quran refers to this meaning:

﴿ وَمِنْ ءَايَتِهِۦٓ أَنْ خَلَقَ لَكُم مِّنْ أَنفُسِكُمْ أَزْوَٰجًا لِّتَسْكُنُوٓا۟ إِلَيْهَا وَجَعَلَ بَيْنَكُم مَّوَدَّةً وَرَحْمَةً ۚ إِنَّ فِي ذَٰلِكَ لَأَيَٰتٍ لِّقَوْمٍ يَتَفَكَّرُونَ ۝ ﴾

{And among His Signs is this, that He created for you mates from among yourselves, that ye may dwell in tranquility with them, and He has put love and mercy between your (hearts): verily in that are Signs for those who reflect.}[36]

Two - He must provide her with the basic and simple things such as adequate housing in which her sanctity is maintained. He also provides her with adequate clothing which protects her from lewdness, and adequate food which nourishes the body. This is all done according to his financial means.

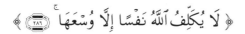

﴿ لَا يُكَلِّفُ ٱللَّهُ نَفْسًا إِلَّا وُسْعَهَا ۚ ۝ ﴾

---

[36] AR-Room: 21

{On no soul doth Allah place a burden greater than it can bear.}[37]

The husband sins by not providing what is needed in the house. The Messenger of Allah's statement, peace be upon him, suffices when he said:

كَفَى بِالمَرْءِ إِثْمًا أَنْ يُضَيِّعَ مَنْ يَقُوتُ

(It is sufficient that a man is considered a sinner if he wastes on what he provides for his family.)[38]

Three - He is to teach her the obligatory aspects of the religion. He instructs her as to what she needs to know from the religion and education. A woman is very susceptible to the religious behavior of her husband. So if she saw him striving for his religion she will see the virtue and worship and desire to do as her husband, seeking his pleasure. If she sees the opposite of this from him, that he doesn't strive at all for his religion; she will do just as he does. Allah has made the wife's protection from the fire a trust by the husband's when He said:

---

[37] Al-Baqarah: 286
[38] Related by Ahmad, Abu Daawud, al-Haakim, and al-Bayhaqi in *as-Sunan*, and as-Suyootee detailed its authenticity.

46

﴿ يَـٰٓأَيُّهَا ٱلَّذِينَ ءَامَنُوا۟ قُوٓا۟ أَنفُسَكُمْ وَأَهْلِيكُمْ نَارًا وَقُودُهَا ٱلنَّاسُ وَٱلْحِجَارَةُ ۝ ﴾

{O ye who believe! Save yourselves and your families from a Fire whose fuel is Men and stones.}[39]

Four - The husband is to be jealous over her, not to be suspicious of her and not tolerate things that dishonor the family or exposes them to evil gossip. So whoever sees or hears of something that dishonors his wife and disregards it, he has removed himself from the group of men who has status with Allah and with the people. The Messenger of Allah, may the peace and blessings of Allah be upon him, said:

أَتَعْجَبُونَ مِنْ غِيْرَةِ سَعْد بْنِ عِبَادَة أَحَدُ الصَّحَابَة وَ اللهِ لَأنا أَغْيَر مِنْهُ وَ اللهُ أَغْيَرُ مِنِّي

(Are you all not amazed by the jealousy of Sa'd bin 'Ubaadah? By Allah, I am more jealous than him and Allah is more jealous than me.)[40]

There are two types of jealousy, praiseworthy jealousy and it is within the limits of moderation. And then there is jealousy that is hated which the Messenger of Allah, may the peace and blessings of Allah be upon him, spoke about in his statement:

مِنَ الْغَيْرَةِ غَيْرَةٌ يُبْغِضُهَا اللهُ عَزَّ وَ جَلَّ وَ هِيَ غَيْرَةُ الرَّجُلِ عَلَى أَهْلِهِ مِنْ غَيْرِ رَيْبَةٍ وَ غَيْرَةٌ يُحِبُّهَا اللهُ وَ هِيَ الْغَيْرَةُ فِي الرَّيْبَةِ

(From the types of jealousy is the jealousy that Allah Almighty hates, and it's the jealousy of man over his family, while being suspicious of them. There is jealousy that Allah loves and it's the jealousy that a man has for his family while not being suspicious of them and trusting them.)[41]

Five - He should be enjoyable with her in the house; being excited to meet her and listen to her when she talks to him. He should joke around and flirt with

---

[40] Related by al-Bukhaaree.
[41] Related by an-Nisaa'ee, Aboo Daawud, Ahmad, Ibn Maajah, ad-Daarimee, and al-Haakim authenticated it.

---

her. Some ignorant people think that playing around with the wife diminishes one's humility and piety. This is a grave mistake and the Messenger of Allah, may the peace and blessings of Allah be upon him, was the most humble servant and leader who ruled by what was revealed to him. He used to race his wife 'Aaishah, may Allah be pleased with her. The Messenger of Allah, may the peace and blessings of Allah be upon him, said:

أَكْمَلُ المُؤْمِنِيْنَ إِيْمَانًا أَحْسَنهِمْ خُلُقًا وَ خِيَارُكُمْ خِيَارُكُمْ لِنِسَائِهِمْ

(The best of the believers who believe are those with the best of manners, and the best of you are those who treat their women well.)[42]

Six - He is to have the best character with her and speak to her with gentleness and overlook some of her mistakes. He should advise her with mildness, and display love and mercy. The Messenger of Allah, peace be upon him, said:

إِنَّ أَحَبَّكُمْ إِلَيَّ أَحَاسنكُمْ أَخْلَاقًا المُوَطَّؤُونَ أَكْنَافًا الَّذِيْنَ يَأْلَفُونَ وَ يُؤْلَفُونَ

---

[42] Related at-Tirmidhee, Ibn Maajah, and al-Haakim, an all authenticated it.

49

(Indeed the most beloved to me from amongst those of you who do good are those with good manners, those who are easy to befriend and do not harm others, and those who befriend the people and are befriended.)[43]

These are the most important rights of the husband over his wife and the wife over the husband. As for the shared rights, the first of them is to bear with everything that comes from each other that may be harmful to one another. Mankind is not infallible, and there is no one who doesn't make mistakes. So the husband bears some harm from his wife and she too bears with him. The wife bears some cruelty from the husband, and it's from the obligatory acts to remind the husband that he should be appreciative of bearing harm from his wife. The woman is emotional and quickly forgets the beauty of her husband. The Messenger of Allah, may the peace and blessings of Allah be upon him, said:

لَوْ أَحْسَنْتَ إِلَى إِحْدَاهُنَّ الدَّهْرَ كُلَّهُ ثُمَّ رَأَتْ مِنْكَ شَيْئًا قَالَتْ مَا رَأَيْتُ
مِنْكَ خَيْرًا قَطْ

---

[43] Related by at-Tabaraanee in as-Sagheer al-Awsat and al-Mundhiree pointed out its weakness.

(If you were always good to one of them all of the time, but then she saw you do something wrong, she would say, "I haven't seen any good from you".)[44]

From the shared obligatory acts, then every husband and wife should feel a sense of shared responsibility towards the house and the family. Meaning, they should both feel that it is upon them to make themselves and their children happy by working together through the trials of life. So, it isn't correct for the husband not to consider his wife's comfort in the house and her work and troubles, and only be concerned with his own comfort at the expense of his wife and children. And it isn't correct for the woman to not consider her husband's workload and the expenses of the house to the point that her only interest is her own comfort at the expense of the husband.

With this, I ask Allah to return those husbands and wives who are astray back to practicing this upright religion, and to grant their families fruition based on the noble Quran, and Allah is the one who grants success.

---

[44] Related by al-Bukhaaree.

Chapter Five: Polygyny in Islam[45]

All praise is for Allah, Lord of all the worlds, may the peace and blessings of Allah be upon Muhammad, the Messenger of Allah. To proceed:

There has been a lot of talk about polygyny; from those who attack Islam are the ones who cast doubts about its validity and resent the religion and its adherents, to the person influenced by the enemies, misinterpreting the Quran and twisting the meanings of the verses and prophetic narrations to give it his own understanding and to fit his desires. The amazing thing is not these two types of people because this is craft of the enemies, the Most High says:

﴿ وَدُّواْ لَوْ تَكْفُرُونَ كَمَا كَفَرُواْ فَتَكُونُونَ سَوَآءً ۚ ﴾ ۝

{They wish that you reject Faith, as they have rejected (Faith), and thus that you all become equal (like one another).}[46]

---

[45] The practice or condition of having more than one wife at one time.

[46] An-Nisaa'a: 89

52

قَضَايَا تَهُمُّ المَرْأَةُ

Issues the Muslim Woman Should Concern Herself With

Rather the amazing thing is the people of knowledge
and religion who have been affected by this kind of
person, misinterpreting the Quran, desiring to follow
the opinion of the enemies so that one can escape
their slander. But does their slander harm us or our
religion, as the poem goes, "Are the clouds harmed
by the barking of the dogs? May the troublemaker be
destroyed!"

The Muslim, and all praise is due to Allah, holds to
his beliefs and does not doubt his religion. He listens
to the words of his Lord and the prophetic
narrations of his Prophet Muhammad, peace be
upon him. Allah the Most High says:

﴿ فَأَنكِحُواْ مَا طَابَ لَكُم مِّنَ ٱلنِّسَآءِ مَثۡنَىٰ
وَثُلَٰثَ وَرُبَٰعَ ۖ ۝ ﴾

*{...Then marry (other) women of your choice, two
or three, or four.}*[47]

---

[47] An-Nisaa'a: 3

قَضَايَا تَهُمُّ المَرْأَةُ
Issues the Muslim Woman Should Concern Herself With

The Prophet, peace and blessings be upon him, ordered the one who converted having many wives, to choose four and divorce the remaining wives, as he commanded *Gheelaan* and others.[48]

This legislation allows more than one of the good qualities contained within the religion. Islam has many good qualities that are fit for both general and specific benefits. Women are in need of one who can support them and establish their needs and spend on them. Women are also afflicted with menstruation and post natal bleeding that happens after birth. If the man fears temptation and falling into illegal sexual intercourse the divine legislation allows him to take other wives due to these great benefits; yet the biased is oblivious to them and the ignorant doesn't understand them. Also when a predicament occurs amongst the women because of something happening to the men either due to war or because of the rise in the number of women, this is from Allah's wisdom as it is related in the narrative from the Prophet, peace be upon him:

فِي آخَرِ الزَّمَانِ يَكُونُ لِخَمْسِيْنَ امْرَأَةٍ القَيِّمِ الوَاحِد

---

[48] Related by Ahmad, at-Tirmidhee, and authenticated by Ibn Hibbaan and al-Haakim.

(In the last days there will be fifty women to one man, who will be responsible for each.)[49]

Or due to the women's incapability and weakness as our Lord points out in His statement:

﴿ ٱلرِّجَالُ قَوَّٰمُونَ عَلَى ٱلنِّسَآءِ بِمَا فَضَّلَ ٱللَّهُ بَعۡضَهُمۡ عَلَىٰ بَعۡضٖ وَبِمَآ أَنفَقُواْ مِنۡ أَمۡوَٰلِهِمۡۚ كَبِيرٗا ﴾

{Men are the protectors and maintainers of women, because Allâh has made one of them to excel the other, and because they spend (to support them) from their means.}[50]

And the statement of the Most High:

﴿ وَلِلرِّجَالِ عَلَيۡهِنَّ دَرَجَةٞۗ ﴾

{...And they (women) have rights (over their husbands as regards living expenses) similar (to

---

[49] Related by al-Bukhaaree, Muslim, and others.
[50] An-Nisaa'a: 34

_____

those of their husbands) over them (as regards
obedience and respect) to what is reasonable, but
men have a degree (of responsibility) over them.)[51]

Islam came accompanied with mercy and
compassion towards the weak such as the woman
and orphan. This was in opposition to the days of
ignorance before Islam, which oppressed the woman
and excluded her from inheritance and prevented
her from marriage. Daughters were buried alive,
some did so out of fear of poverty while others did
this to their daughters specifically for fear of
dishonor. Islam came prohibiting oppression and
transgression informing people that all provisions
were from Allah as the Most High says:

﴿ وَلَا تَقْتُلُوٓاْ أَوْلَٰدَكُمْ خَشْيَةَ إِمْلَٰقٖ نَّحْنُ نَرْزُقُهُمْ وَإِيَّاكُمْ إِنَّ
قَتْلَهُمْ كَانَ خِطْـٔٗا كَبِيرٗا ۝ ﴾

{And kill not your children for fear of poverty. We
provide for them and for you. Surely, the killing of
them is a great sin.)[52]

_____

[51] Al-Baqarah: 228

Therefore Allah, *al-Hayy* (the Ever Living), *al-Qayyum* (The Self-Subsisting) provides for all. However, man has been commanded to work and spend from his means. If he fears being unjust amongst wives then he should limit himself to only one. The Most High says:

$$\text{﴿ فَإِنْ خِفْتُمْ أَلَّا تَعْدِلُواْ فَوَٰحِدَةً ۞ ﴾}$$

{...But if you fear that you shall not be able to deal justly (with them), then only one}[53]

And polygyny was present in the previous divine legislations that Allah revealed. Prophet *Sulaymaan* (Solomon), peace be upon him, once said, "At night I will go to ninety of my wives so that each one will have a child to fight in the path of Allah."[54]

This is a mercy from Allah for His servants. He legislated polygyny and allowed specific circumstances for our Prophet Muhammad, peace be upon him, as he was permitted more than four to

---

[52] Al-Israa'a: 31
[53] An-Nisaa'a: 3
[54] Related by al-Bukhaaree and Muslim.

---

establish connections based on the religion and upon the establishment of the Islamic state.

Polygyny is only opposed by a stubborn person or one who harbors enmity, one who desires to weaken the Muslim offspring or wants the people to fall into adultery as it has occurred in other countries. I ask Allah to pardon us and them in this life and in the hereafter. By Allah, they know the benefits of polygyny but they shut their eyes to it in order to defame the religion or to commit illegal sexual intercourse amongst the Muslims. Allah is wiser and more knowledgeable to legislate for His servants what will benefit them and prevent them from harming themselves such as adultery, sex out of wedlock, oppression, and transgression. May the peace and blessings of Allah be upon our Prophet Muhammad and upon his family and companions.[55]

---

[55] Written by: *Ash-Shaykh* 'Abdur-Rahmaan bin 'Abdillah Aali Faryaan

---

Chapter Six: The Head Covering of the Muslim Woman[56]

All praise is for Allah, alone. May peace and blessings be upon him who there will never be another Prophet after, and upon his family and his companions. To proceed:

It is known to everyone familiar with an affliction that has recently become widespread; *at-Tabarruj* (Muslim women displaying their beauty i.e. a part of the body or decorated clothing), *as-Sufoor* (Muslim women leaving out totally uncovered), and not wearing the proper head covering around men. Many display their beauty that they have been prohibited from displaying. No doubt, this is from the greatest of evil deeds and open acts of disobedience. And there is no doubt that it is one of the greatest causes for afflictions to occur and for (Allah's) punishment to be carried out (on the people). Immorality and shamelessness, sins, and

---

[56] This is a section from a treatise regarding the Muslim Woman's Head-Cover by *ash-Shaykh* 'Abdul-'Azeez bin 'Abdillah bin Baaz –may Allah have mercy upon him.

---

the prevalence of corruption are all direct results of *at-Tabarruj* and *as-Sufoor*.

Therefore Muslims you must fear Allah, deal with the foolish (who call to the prohibited) and prevent your women from what Allah has prohibited them from. Have them observe the proper head and body covering. Beware of Allah's anger and know that His punishment is great. It has been authentically reported from the Prophet, peace be upon him, that he said:

إِنَّ النَّاسَ إِذَا رَأَوْا المُنْكَرَ فَلَمْ يُغَيِّرُوهُ أَوْشَكَ أَنْ يَعمهم اللهُ بِعِقَابِهِ

(When the people see *al-Munkar* (every sinful and objectionable thing) but they do not change it, Allah will envelope all of them with His punishment.)[57]

Allah, the Glorified has commanded the women to cover in His noble book, and to stay in their homes. He has warned them from *at-Tabarruj* (to display something of beauty such as a part of the body or decorated clothing) and speaking with a soft and sexy voice to men as a means of protecting them from

---

[57] Related by Aboo Daawud, at-Tirmidhee, and an-Nisaa'ee with authentic chains of transmission.

---

seduction and as a warning from the causes of temptation. The Most High says:

﴿ يَٰنِسَآءَ ٱلنَّبِيِّ لَسْتُنَّ كَأَحَدٍ مِّنَ ٱلنِّسَآءِ إِنِ ٱتَّقَيْتُنَّ فَلَا تَخْضَعْنَ بِٱلْقَوْلِ فَيَطْمَعَ ٱلَّذِى فِى قَلْبِهِۦ مَرَضٌ وَقُلْنَ قَوْلًا مَّعْرُوفًا ۝ وَقَرْنَ فِى بُيُوتِكُنَّ وَلَا تَبَرَّجْنَ تَبَرُّجَ ٱلْجَٰهِلِيَّةِ ٱلْأُولَىٰ وَأَقِمْنَ ٱلصَّلَوٰةَ وَءَاتِينَ ٱلزَّكَوٰةَ وَأَطِعْنَ ٱللَّهَ وَرَسُولَهُۥٓ إِنَّمَا يُرِيدُ ٱللَّهُ لِيُذْهِبَ عَنكُمُ ٱلرِّجْسَ أَهْلَ ٱلْبَيْتِ وَيُطَهِّرَكُمْ تَطْهِيرًا ۝ ﴾

{O Consorts of the Prophet! ye are not like any of the (other) women: if ye do fear (Allah), be not too complaisant of speech, lest one in whose heart is a disease should be moved with desire: but speak ye a speech (that is) just. And stay quietly in your houses, and make not a dazzling display, like that of the former Times of Ignorance: and establish Regular Prayer, and give Regular Charity; and obey Allah and His Messenger. And Allah only wishes to

---

*remove all abomination from you, ye Members of
the Family, and to make you pure and spotless.*[58]

In this verse the Glorious prohibited the wives of the
noble Prophet, the mother of the believers who are
the best and purest women from speaking seductively
to men lest one in whose heart is a disease should be
moved with the desire of adultery. He commands
them to stay in their homes. He prohibits them from
the *Tabarruj* of *al-Jaahiliyyah* (pre-Islamic period)
which was the display of their beauty and body such
as the hair, face, neck, chest, arms, feet, etc. This is
due to the great corruption and tribulation that it
contained in addition to moving men's hearts in
pursuing the ways to adultery. And when Allah the
Glorified warned the mother of the believers from
these evil things along with what would rectify and
purify them, they changed one by one due to the
warning, the rejection of sins, and fear for (falling
into) the causes of tribulation. May Allah protect us
and you from the deviances of the tribulations. It
proves the generality of the ruling applying to them
as well as other women, His statement in this verse:

---

[58] Al-Ahzaab: 32 -33

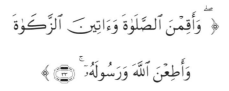

{...and they establish Regular Prayer, and give Regular Charity; and obey Allah and His Messenger.}

These commands are general rulings applied to the wives of the Prophet, peace be upon him, and to others. The Mighty and Majestic says:

﴿ وَإِذَا سَأَلْتُمُوهُنَّ مَتَٰعًا فَسْـَٔلُوهُنَّ مِن وَرَآءِ حِجَابٍ ۚ ذَٰلِكُمْ أَطْهَرُ لِقُلُوبِكُمْ وَقُلُوبِهِنَّ ۚ ۝ ﴾

{And when ye ask (his ladies) for anything ye want ask them from before a screen: that makes for greater purity for your hearts and for theirs.}[59]

---

[59] Al-Ahzaab: 53

63

This noble verse is a clear text that clarifies the obligation for women to cover their hair in front of men as well as covering the rest of their body. Allah the Glorified has clarified in this verse that covering is a greater purity for the hearts of the men and will keep them from falling into immodesty and its causes. The Glorified points out that uncovering the head and not wearing it is impure and filthy. He also points out that wearing the head cover is purity and a means of preservation. Therefore Muslim men educate (your family) with the conduct that Allah has shown you. Obey the commands of Allah. Make your women wear the head covering which will be a cause for purification and the way to success. The Most High says:

﴿ يَـٰٓأَيُّهَا ٱلنَّبِىُّ قُل لِّأَزْوَٰجِكَ وَبَنَاتِكَ وَنِسَآءِ ٱلْمُؤْمِنِينَ يُدْنِينَ عَلَيْهِنَّ مِن جَلَـٰبِيبِهِنَّ ذَٰلِكَ أَدْنَىٰٓ أَن يُعْرَفْنَ فَلَا يُؤْذَيْنَ وَكَانَ ٱللَّهُ غَفُورًا رَّحِيمًا ۝ ﴾

{O Prophet! tell thy wives and daughters, and the believing women, that they should cast their outer

64

garments over their persons (when abroad): that is most convenient, that they should be known (as such) and not molested. And Allah is Oft-Forgiving, Most Merciful.[60]

The word al-Jalaabeeb in this verse is plural for Jilbaab. The Jilbaab is that which the woman places over her head to cover it and conceal the rest of her body. Allah the Glorious has commanded all of the wives of the believers to cast their garments over their beauty; the hair, face, etc. This is so that they will be recognized with modesty and not tease (men) and have men hit on them and molest them. The Most High says:

﴿ قُل لِّلْمُؤْمِنِينَ يَغُضُّوا۟ مِنْ أَبْصَٰرِهِمْ وَيَحْفَظُوا۟ فُرُوجَهُمْ ۚ ذَٰلِكَ أَزْكَىٰ لَهُمْ ۗ إِنَّ ٱللَّهَ خَبِيرٌۢ بِمَا يَصْنَعُونَ ۝ وَقُل لِّلْمُؤْمِنَٰتِ يَغْضُضْنَ مِنْ أَبْصَٰرِهِنَّ وَيَحْفَظْنَ فُرُوجَهُنَّ وَلَا يُبْدِينَ زِينَتَهُنَّ إِلَّا مَا ظَهَرَ مِنْهَا ۖ ۝ ﴾

---

[60] Al-Ahzaab: 59

{Say to the believing men that they should lower their gaze and guard their modesty: that will make for greater purity for them: and Allah is well acquainted with all that they do. And say to the believing women that they should lower their gaze and guard their modesty; that they should not display their beauty and ornaments except what (must ordinarily) appear thereof.}[61]

In these two noble verses, Allah commands the believing men and women to lower their gaze and guard their modesty. This is to prevent the chances of adultery from happening and the great calamities that occur amongst the Muslims as a direct result of it. This is because staring lustfully is a sickness of the heart and a shameless act of obscenity. Lowering the gaze is a way to avoid falling into this vice. Lowering the gaze and guarding modesty is purer for the believer in this life and in the hereafter. Looking lustfully is from the greatest causes of ruin and punishment in this life and in the hereafter. We ask Allah for pardon from that.

---

[61] An-Noor: 30-31

It is known that showing the face and palms cause corruption and tribulation. The proof is what has been established from 'Aaishah, may Allah be pleased with her, in the story of the slander that she covered her face when she heard the voice of Safwaan bin al-Mu'attal as-Sulmee. She said that he knew what she looked like before the head covering was legislated. Therefore this indicates that women after the verse of revelation known as *Aayat-ul-Hijaab* came down were not known due to their lower garments and faces being covered. It is obvious in today's times that the women have been afflicted with the spread of displaying their beauty. Therefore it is obligatory to prevent excuses and stop the vast means that lead to corruption and the appearance of obscenities. From the greatest causes of corruption is men being alone with women and travelling with them without a *Mahram*. It has been authenticated that the Prophet, peace be upon him, said:

لَا تُسَافِرُ امْرَأَةٌ إِلاَّ مَعَ ذِيْ مَحْرَمٍ وَ لَا يَخْلُون رَجُلٌ بِامْرَأَةٍ إِلاَّ وَ مَعَهَا ذُو مَحْرَمٍ

(A woman does not travel unless accompanied by a *Mahram* (male relative escort), and a man and a

67

woman are not alone together unless there is a
Mahram with her.)[62]

And he, peace be upon him said:

لَا يَخْلُونَ رَجُلٌ بِامْرَأَةٍ فَـإِنَّ الشَّيْطَانَ ثَالِثُهُمَا

(A man and a woman are not alone together as a
couple except that the *Shaytaan* (Satan) is third one
to accompany them.)[63]

And he, peace be upon him, said:

لَا يَبِيتَنَّ رَجُلٌ عِنْدَ امْرَأَةٍ إِلَّا أَنْ يَكُونَ زَوْجًا أَوْ ذَا مَحْرَمٍ

(A man does not spend the night in a home with a
woman unless her husband or *Mahram* is present.)[64]

So fear Allah Muslims and be responsible for your
women and prevent them from what Allah has
prohibited them from, such as uncovering,
displaying their beauty, showing off parts of the

---

[62] Related by al-Bukhaaree and Muslim.
[63] Related by Ahmad, at-Tirmidhee, and authenticated by al-
Haakim.
[64] Related by Muslim in his *Saheeh*.

---

body, and imitating Allah's enemies; the Christians and whoever else they may imitate. Know that staying quiet about it is the same as taking part in it. It causes sins and the anger of Allah to occur and for His punishment to prevail. May He pardon us and all of you from its evil.

And from the greatest obligations (of enjoining the good and forbidding the evil) is warning men from being alone with women, entering their homes when they are alone, travelling with them while no *Mahram* is present. All of these are causes of tribulation and corruption. It has been authentically reported that the Prophet, peace be upon him, said:

مَا تَرَكْتُ بَعْدِي فِتْنَةً أَضَرَّ عَلَى الرِّجَالِ مِنَ النِّسَاء

(I have not left a trial after me more harmful upon men than women.)[65]

And from the greatest corruptions that occur are Muslim women imitating the non-Muslim Christian women and their like. Imitating them in wearing short clothes, displaying the hair and outer beauty, combing their hair like the people of disbelief and

---

[65] Agreed upon.

69

---

disobedience, adding extensions, and wearing manufactured hair known as *al-Baarookah*. The Prophet, peace be upon him, said:

مَنْ تَشَبَّهَ بِقَوْمٍ فَهُوَ مِنْـهُم

(Whoever imitates a people then he is from them.)[66]

It is well known what results from this form of imitation and these short clothes which make the woman appear naked (even though they have on clothes), results such as corruption, temptation, abandonment of the religion, and shamelessness. Therefore it is obligatory to intently focus on warning from all of it, and to prevent the women from it and to be stern because its consequences, its inclination, and its corruption are great. It is not permissible to be easy on the young girls since their cultivation will lead them to being accustomed to covering. If not they will dislike it when they get older causing them to fall into demoralization, the prohibited, and tribulation that is feared for the older women to fall into.

---

[66] Related by Ahmad, Aboo Daawud, and others. And authenticated by Ibn Hibbaan.

So fear Allah, servants of Allah! Warn (the people) from what Allah has prohibited you from and cooperate with one another on piety and righteousness. Enjoin one another with the truth and to be patient. Know that Allah the Glorious will ask you all about this and either reward or punish you all of your deeds and He the Glorified is the patient and with the righteous, and with those who do good deeds. Be patient and fear Allah and do good deeds. Indeed Allah loves those who do good deeds.

I ask Allah to help His religion and raise His word and rectify the rulers. That He obliterate corruption among them and aide them in the truth and rectify the inner-self. That He will make us, you, and all of the Muslims successful. And that He will rectify the servants and their countries in this life and in the hereafter. Indeed He is able to do all and worthy of responding (to this supplication). Allah is sufficient for us and is the best of those entrusted. There is no strength or power except with Allah the Most High, the Great. And may the peace and blessings of Allah be upon Muhammad and upon his family and all of his companions.

Chapter Seven: An Explanation of the Rulings for the Wife mourning the loss of her Husband[67]

One- She must stay in the home where she lived with her husband when he passes away. She does not go out from it unless there is a need or a dire necessity such as going to the hospital due to illness and buying the things she needs from the market like bread, etc. This is only if she does not have anyone to do these things for her.

Two- She avoids wearing alluring clothing.

Three- She avoids all of types of perfume unless she has come off of her menses in which case there is no harm in her applying some scent.

Four- She avoids wearing jewelry made of gold, silver, diamonds, or anything else, whether it is necklaces, pearls, etc.

---

[67] Written by: General President for the Administration for Knowledge-Based Research and Legal Rulings, Missionary Work, and Guidance; 'Abdul-'Azeez bin Baaz

---

Five- She avoids wearing *al-Kohl* because the Messenger of Allah, peace be upon him, forbade the mourning woman from all of these things. She can wash with water, soap, and lotus whenever she wants. She can speak with her relatives and women whenever she wants. She can sit with her male relatives that she is not allowed to marry (such as the brother, uncle, nephew, son, etc.) and serve them coffee and food. She can work in her house, house's garden, and the porches night and day, doing all of the various types of housework like cooking, sewing, sweeping, washing clothes, milking the animals, etc. She can do everything the woman who is not mourning does. She can walk in the moonlight without her face covered like other women and she can toss her face cover over her head when she does not have a non relative chaperon. May the peace and blessings of Allah be upon our Prophet Muhammad and upon his family and companions.

Chapter Eight: The Dangers of Intermingling

All praise is for Allah, and may peace and blessings be upon His Messenger. To proceed: Indeed the most dangerous of affairs that Allah has warned the Muslims from is mixing of the sexes, both male and female. That is because it is one of the greatest causes that easily can lead to obscenity. Even more dangerous than that, is the seclusion of a woman with a man who is not her *Mahram*. This is a means for *Shaytaan* to enter. The Prophet, peace be upon him, said:

لَا يَخْلُونَ رَجُلٌ بِامْرَأَةٍ فَـإِنَّ الشَّيْطَانَ ثَالِثُهُمَا

(A man and a woman are not alone together as a couple except that the *Shaytaan* (Satan) is third one to accompany them.)[68]

The reality of seclusion is that a man is alone with a woman in absence of people. This happens a lot in many Muslim homes where some have taken maids

---

[68] Related by Ahmad, at-Tirmidhee, and authenticated by al-Haakim.

---

from foreign countries to work for the family, the home, and in public. They are brought from far off places without proper male escorts. It is well known that a lot of time the man of the house or one of the male members of the family is alone with these maids. Whenever the family goes out the plot of *Shaytaan* comes about. It is a plot that manifests the danger that the Messenger of Allah, peace be upon him, informed of. The previous narration includes all men even if they are righteous or old.

Likewise this includes the woman whether she is righteous or old. This is something that is viewed as being from the natural human inclination that men have towards women especially when many of these servants are young beautiful women. Because of this we consider bringing foreign maids into the homes very dangerous. The Muslims have been tested by this today. We ask Allah to protect them from its evil and to guide the rulers to rectify the issue before it is out of control.

There is another form of mixing that some of the Muslims have been tested with. Its danger is by no means lesser than the last issue. It is the hiring of a foreign male driver. We see them come and go with

---

their families and being alone with them without proper male relative escorts. We have been assured that a group of the Muslims have begun sending their daughters to school with the driver or sending one of the female relatives to the store alone with the driver. He may be non-Muslim or a deviant in his practice of the religion, his manners, or in his appearance, but the righteous man is the one who must be chosen. This is forbidden based on the previous narration as evil is likely to happen. The wise Muslim does not accept this happening to his family and it is not permissible for him to neglect this trust. He should protect the most precious thing that he possesses which are his female relatives from this great danger.

How many horrible stories do we hear of because of this type of laxness and neglect in repelling the love of affluence and arrogance?

My Muslim brother...My Muslim sister...Islam is strict concerning the issue of being alone with relatives that are not male relatives like the female maternal and paternal cousin. The Prophet, peace be upon him, said:

إِيَّاكُمْ وَ الدُّخُولَ عَلَى النِّسَاءِ

(Beware of entering the homes when the women are alone.)

So a man asked, "What about the brother-in-law O Messenger of Allah?" He responded:

الحَمُو المَوْتُ

(The in-law is death.)[69]

The meaning (of this statement) is to warn from mixing with women and being alone with the male relatives that are not considered permissible male relative escorts. The greatest types of seclusion are the relatives of the husband being left alone with the wife; relatives such as the husband's brother, his nephew, his uncle, and his male cousins, etc. All of these are relatives who are not considered male relative escorts for her, whether on a journey or just going out. Just as we warn the Muslim women from travelling with male relatives who are not considered male relative escorts. The Messenger, peace be upon him, said:

---

[69] Related by al-Bukhaaree and Muslim.

لاَ تُسَافِرِ المَرْأَةِ إِلاَّ مَعَ ذِي مَحْرَمٍ

(A woman does not travel unless accompanied by a *Mahram* (male relative escort).)[70]

We also warn the Muslims from mixing the male and female children even if they are brothers and sisters after reaching the age of distinction. They should be separated from sleeping with one another as the Prophet, peace be upon him, used to command this.[71]

Based on what has preceded we know the dangers of mixing the sexes regardless of the circumstances whether at home or outside. Allah Most High says:

﴿ يَٰٓأَيُّهَا ٱلَّذِينَ ءَامَنُواْ لَا تَدْخُلُواْ بُيُوتًا غَيْرَ بُيُوتِكُمْ حَتَّىٰ تَسْتَأْنِسُواْ وَتُسَلِّمُواْ عَلَىٰٓ أَهْلِهَا ۚ ٢٧ ﴾

---

[70] Related by al-Bukhaaree and Muslim.
[71] In a narration that was related by Ahmad and Aboo Daawud.

{O ye who believe! enter not houses other than your own, until ye have asked permission and saluted those in them.}[72]

Therefore we consider those who bring women from abroad here and allow them to mix with their children or those who bring men from abroad and they mix with their women, they have exposed themselves and their families to the greatest forms of danger. They place all of society at risk due to this negligence and cause them to fall into the prostitution that the Prophet, peace be upon him, said:

لاَ يَدْخُلُ الجَنَّةَ دَيُوث

(ad-Dayooth, (the one who allows his women to go outside uncovered) will not enter paradise.)[73]

The one who allows his women to go out uncovered (ad-Dayooth) is one who is pleased with his family's involvement with indecency. It is something expected with this type of negligence. Due to this

---

[72] An-Noor: 27
[73] Related by an-Nisaa'ee, al-Bazzaar, and al-Haakim who authenticated it.

Muslim brother, we suggest you keep away from this issue. Just as we suggest (you remember) Allah the Glorified is a watcher over everything and fear the day of standing before Him, a day your daughter and sister will stand before Allah, the day of resurrection, where they will be held to account (for what they did):

﴿ يَوْمَ لَا يَنفَعُ مَالٌ وَلَا بَنُونَ ۝ إِلَّا مَنْ أَتَى ٱللَّهَ بِقَلْبٍ سَلِيمٍ ۝ ﴾

{The Day whereon neither wealth nor sons will avail, But only he (will prosper) that brings to Allah a sound heart.}[74]

And understand His statement, the Glorified:

﴿ يَٰٓأَيُّهَا ٱلَّذِينَ ءَامَنُوا۟ لَا تَخُونُوا۟ ٱللَّهَ وَٱلرَّسُولَ وَتَخُونُوٓا۟ أَمَٰنَٰتِكُمْ وَأَنتُمْ تَعْلَمُونَ ۝ ﴾

---

[74] Ash-Shu'araa: 88-89

{O ye that believe! betray not the trust of Allah and the Messenger, nor misappropriate knowingly things entrusted to you.}[75]

Whenever you are compelled to employ a maid then do not hire her unless she is a Muslim and her husband accompanies her. Ensure that they both have a separate place that is isolated from your home. You must choose a maid who is older in age and pious.

As for the foreign male drivers then we suggest you rely on yourself or one of your older sons. Whenever you are compelled to get a driver then you must accompany them or have one of the male relative escorts accompany them and be careful not to trust them. The issue is not easy but do not allow them into your home while you are away.

My Muslim brother, be careful of these female non-Muslim educators who you have entrusted your children to, perhaps they may educate your sons upon a path that is not upright.

---

[75] Al-Anfaal: 27

قَضَايَا تَهُمُّ المَرْأَةُ
Issues the Muslim Woman Should Concern Herself With

My Muslim brother, it is not permissible for you to shake hands with a woman you are not married to. It is not permissible to look at women you are not an escort for. Allah has ordered you to lower your gaze whether it be men or women just as it is not permissible for the Muslim woman to uncover her face or any part of the body in front of foreign men.

My Muslim sister, beware of the dangers of at-Tabarruj and displaying your beauty to non-relative males. Beware of always going out without any need as Allah the Most High says:

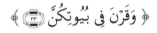

{And stay quietly in your houses.}

Chapter Nine: The Descriptions of the Women of Paradise and the Description of the Women of the Hellfire

Sister in Islam, we are saying this specifically for you since you represent a portion of society and educate the other half, and because the enemies of Islam have focused on you; desiring (your) elimination and division, all in the name of freedom.

Sister in Islam, I will show you the descriptions of the women of paradise and the descriptions of the women of the hellfire. You can choose the path (you want to follow). The Most High says:

﴿ فَلَا تَخْضَعْنَ بِٱلْقَوْلِ فَيَطْمَعَ ٱلَّذِى فِى قَلْبِهِۦ مَرَضٌ وَقُلْنَ قَوْلًا مَّعْرُوفًا ۝ وَقَرْنَ فِى بُيُوتِكُنَّ وَلَا تَبَرَّجْنَ تَبَرُّجَ ٱلْجَٰهِلِيَّةِ ٱلْأُولَىٰ وَأَقِمْنَ ٱلصَّلَوٰةَ وَءَاتِينَ ٱلزَّكَوٰةَ وَأَطِعْنَ ٱللَّهَ وَرَسُولَهُۥ ۝ ﴾

قَضَايَا تَهُمُّ الْمَرْأَةُ

Issues the Muslim Woman Should Concern Herself With

{Then be not soft in speech, lest he in whose heart is a disease (of hypocrisy, or evil desire for adultery) should be moved with desire, but speak in an honorable manner. And stay in your houses, and do not display yourselves like that of the times of ignorance, and perform As-Salât (Iqamât-as-Salât), and give Zakât and obey Allâh and His Messenger.}[76]

{Then be not soft in speech...} means to observe piety and that the Muslim woman should keep her voice low in front of men that she is not related to. She should not smile in front of them or joke with them as it will cause men to be moved with desire. *{And stay in your houses...}* Remain within your homes, sisters. The woman should stay in her home as it is better for her. Do not move about with the men or constantly go out of the home unless there is a need. When you go out because of a need then go out modestly. At-Tabarruj[77] is to display something of

---

[76] Al-Ahzaab: 32-33

[77] **T.N. Note:** The definition of the word *at-Tabarruj* is mentioned by the author of *Lisaan-ul-'Arab* (3/33) as the display of a woman's beauty, the uncovering of her face and the attractive qualities of her body in front of men in addition to everything that arouses their desires, and strutting while

_____

beauty such as a part of the body or decorated clothing. Exposing the arms from the over-garment is a form of *at-Tabarruj*. Exposing some of the feet, neck, hair, or detailed portion of clothing underneath is also a form of *at-Tabarruj* such as the pants or the inner transparent clothes. Likewise, gold and perfume and all other decorations (displayed) in front of non-related men is a form of *at-Tabarruj*.

As for the women of the hellfire then the Messenger of Allah, peace be upon him, described them in a prophetic narration:

وَ نِسَاءٌ كَاسِيَاتٌ عَارِيَاتٌ مُمِيلاَتٌ مَائِلاَتٌ رُءُوسُهُنَّ كَأَسْنِمَةِ البُخْتِ المَائِلَةِ لاَ يَدْخُلْنَ الجَنَّة وَ لاَ يَجِدْنَ رِيْحَهَا

(...women clothed yet naked, misguided while leading others astray, their heads were like the humps of the long necked camels leaning to one side. They will not enter paradise nor will they smell its fragrance.)

_____

observing a type of walk which is done exclusively for anyone besides her husband.

The phrase كَاسِيَاتٌ *Kaasiyaat* (Clothed women), عَارِيَاتٌ *Aaariyaat* (Naked women) means that they wear clothes but they are not covered properly or that they are devoid of modesty. The phrase مَائِلاتٌ *Maailaat* (misguided) مُمِيْلاتٌ *Mumeelaat* (while leading others astray) means deviant from the straight path (of Islam) and modesty and that they are infected with sick hearts. The phrase رُءُوسُهُنَّ كَأَسْنِمَةِ البُخْتِ *Ru'oosuhunna Ka'Asnimat-il-Bukht* means they do their hair like the humps of the long necked camels.

Sister in Islam, we have showed you a picture of the descriptions of the women of paradise and a picture of the women of hellfire so choose any of the two paths.

Sister in Islam, have a set limit for your educational studies and do not ignore marriage over it. By forsaking it you may become a widow of the future (an unmarried woman). Do not imitate the dress, manners, and customs of the non-Muslims and do not take them as an example. May Allah protect you from the evil of your enemies, who lurk for you, and may blessings be upon Muhammad.

Chapter Ten: Save yourselves and your families from the Hellfire

All praise is for Allah who commands justice and goodness, and who prohibits indecency, sin, lewdness, and disobedience. I bear witness that there is nothing worthy of worship except for Allah alone and that He has no partner, the One to whom everything is subject to. And I bear witness that Muhammad is His servant and His messenger, the one who said:

كُلُّكُمْ رَاعٍ وَ كُلُّكُمْ مَسْؤُولٌ عَنْ رَعِيَّتِهِ

(All of you are a shepherd over your flock and all of you will be asked about your flock.)[78]

May the peace and blessings of Allah be upon his family, and companions. To proceed: People, fear Allah and obey Him. Do good deeds as you will find them on the day when it will be displayed before you. Servants of Allah, the Most High says:

---

[78] Agreed upon.

﴿ يَـٰٓأَيُّهَا ٱلَّذِينَ ءَامَنُوا۟ قُوٓا۟ أَنفُسَكُمْ وَأَهْلِيكُمْ نَارًا وَقُودُهَا

ٱلنَّاسُ وَٱلْحِجَارَةُ عَلَيْهَا مَلَـٰٓئِكَةٌ غِلَاظٌ شِدَادٌ لَّا يَعْصُونَ ٱللَّهَ

مَآ أَمَرَهُمْ وَيَفْعَلُونَ مَا يُؤْمَرُونَ ۝ ﴾

{O ye who believe! Save yourselves and your families from a Fire whose fuel is Men and Stones, over which are (appointed) angels stern (and) severe, who flinch not (from executing) the Commands they receive from Allah, but do (precisely) what they are commanded.}[79]

Servants of Allah, this noble verse requires the head of every family to be mindful and easy on his family, in his manners with them, and in the education and upbringing of his daughters and wives, and anyone else he has authority over. The man of the house guides his family to what will improve them.

He prevents their destruction and protects them and himself from the torment of the fire; we seek refuge in Allah from it. The statement of the Most High,

---

[79] At-Tahreem: 6

{Save yourselves}, is in the form of a command which indicates that it is an obligatory act. So whoever commands his family and guides them to what is good and steers them to obey Allah the Glorified, while forbidding them from disobeying Allah, then he has fulfilled this obligatory act that Allah the Glorified, the Most High has commanded him with. He will find his reward in greater need of being rewarded by Allah.

Whoever neglects his family, not enjoining the good or forbidding the evil, allowing them to do as they please, willingly or negligently, then he has abandoned the fulfillment of this obligatory act. He has exposed himself and his family to the punishment of the hellfire, the promised torment for the one who does not act in accordance with what this noble verse necessitates. We would then understand the obligation of commanding the family to do good deeds and forbidding them from evil deeds contained within this noble verse. The Messenger, may the peace and blessing of Allah be upon him, said:

صِنَفَان مِنْ أَهْل النَّار لَمْ أَرَهمَا : قوْمٌ مَعَهُمْ سِيَاطٌ كَأَذْنَابِ البَقْر يَضْرِبُوْنَ بهَا النَّاسَ وَ نِسَاءٌ كَاسِيَاتٌ عَارِيَاتٌ مُمِيْلاتٌ مَائِلاتٌ

رُءُوسُهُنَّ كَأَسْنِمَةِ البُخْتِ المَائِلَةِ لاَ يَدْخُلْنَ الجَنَّةَ وَ لاَ يَجِدْنَ رِيْحَهَا وَ
إن رِيْحهَا لَيُوجَد مِنْ مَسِيْرة كَذَا وَ كَذَا

(There were two types of people from the inhabitants of the Hellfire that I had never seen before. The first was a group of people with whips like the tails of cows in which they struck the people with. The second were women clothed yet naked, misguided while leading others astray, their heads were like the humps of the long necked camels leaning to one side. They will not enter paradise nor will they smell its fragrance. If they would have smelled it the presence of its distance would be like this and like this.)[80]

We will now deal with the words contained within this narration concerning the second category. The meaning of the word *"Kaasiyaat"* is that they wear clothes but they are naked at the same time, which means that what they are wearing isn't sufficient enough. Either because it is see-through, not properly covering, or it is tight and shows the upper and lower parts of the body or either because she wears it in a way that doesn't cover her properly.

---

[80] Related by Muslim.

The meaning of "*Maailaat*" is 'those who deviate from obedience'. The meaning of "*Mumeelaat*" is 'they steer the hearts of men toward temptation'. The Prophet of Allah, may the peace and blessings of Allah be upon him, has informed us, and he doesn't speak from his own desires, that these types of women will be in the hellfire and will not smell the fragrance of Paradise.

The previous noble verse addresses the believers to save themselves and their families from the fire. So what is it that will make this group of women enter the hellfire as it was stated in the narration? Their guardians were negligent and left them on their own (without guidance). He says *{O you who believe}* which proves that this command describes the characteristics of the believers even if one detested this noble characteristic and exposed himself and his family to the fire, we seek refuge with Allah from it, this is what has been revealed in the noble verse.

As for the narration previously mentioned, if we discussed the reality in light of our women (in today's times) then our discussion will become too lengthy. We find that (most of what is found within this narration) applies to them except for the one

---

whom Allah has guided. However, we will discuss one of their characteristics that they do customarily or stylishly.

It is present amongst the teenage girls and those who speak for the youth amongst them who have no modesty, except for the one whom Allah has guided, where they take a head covering and wrap it around their head. This dear Muslims is a very bad and reprehensible habit which is unacceptable to the believer religiously, modestly or intelligently. It is done from lack of having any of these characteristics. If one practices this custom (of being clothed yet naked as found in the narration), she is covered but the garment she wears still makes her appear naked. That is because the presence of this garment is like it is not really on her, the adornments of her clothes are plainly visible and it shows everyone the shape of her body.

Servant of Allah, Allah the Glorified, the Most High addressed the mothers of the believers, the pure and free from every bad trait and from the best generation of men and women, as indicated by what has been revealed where the Most High said to them:

﴿ فَلَا تَخْضَعْنَ بِٱلْقَوْلِ فَيَطْمَعَ ٱلَّذِى فِى قَلْبِهِۦ مَرَضٌ ۝ ﴾

{If ye do fear (Allah), be not too complaisant of speech, lest one in whose heart is a disease should be moved with desire.}[81]

Meaning: don't speak to men with a soft and low voice because it will entice the immoral and lewd men to be invited to commit obscenity. Therefore, this speech (directed to the mothers of the believers), O servants of Allah, positively perfected the women of this nation. Regarding the generations it is the best of them. The causes of immoral acts were fewer than in any other century. So what is the opinion of a woman in this day and age if she wore clothes that were adorned and raised her outer garment halfway and pulled on both sides of it and passed through men or mixed with them in the marketplaces? If it's one who has a sickness in his heart when he sees her he will be enticed by her and consider her his object of desire. She is the one who caused sin for herself and for her guardian, the one responsible for her in front of Allah on the Day of Judgment. He didn't

---

[81] Al-Ahzaab: 32

---

protect her or himself from the hellfire which was mentioned in the previous noble verse.

Therefore fear Allah, servants of Allah, and maintain and protect the women. Included in the meaning of this phrase is education, advice, adherence, etc. The woman, whether she is intelligent or educated, needs the care and guardianship of a man and for him to look after her with regards to enjoining the good and forbidding the evil. If the believing woman was directed towards and knew the truth she would strive never to leave it. If she only knew that the Prophet, may the peace and blessings of Allah be upon him, called lustfully looking at a woman one is not married to a form of adultery. He said:

كُتِبَ عَلَى ابْنِ آدَمَ نَصِيبُهُ مِن الزِّنَى مُدْرِكٌ ذَلِكَ لاَ مَحَالَة فَزِنَى
العَيْنَيْنِ النَّظَرِ

(The son of Adam has his portion of adultery that he will commit already written down for him. There will be no escape from it. And the adultery of the eyes is the lustful look.)[82]

---

[82] Agreed upon by al-Bukhaaree and Muslim.

If she understood that, if she fits the characteristics
that are mentioned (in the previous narration) and
she still goes to the marketplace (dressed
inappropriately), then she (must also understand
that) she is the primary cause for this type of adultery
(the adultery of the eyes) to occur. That is because
she teased the men into looking at the beauty that
she left exposed. If she understood all of this, then
she would leave off this habit and seek forgiveness
from Allah, from the time of leaving her house to go
to the marketplace until the time she returns. How
many times does this type of adultery happen? We
ask Allah to guide us all, men and women, and show
us the real truth and enable us to follow it, and to
expose falsehood and enable us to stay away from it.
Fear Allah O servant of Allah, follow the things you
were commanded to do and stay away from the
things that you were warned against.

﴿ فَلَا تَغُرَّنَّكُمُ ٱلۡحَيَوٰةُ ٱلدُّنۡيَا وَلَا يَغُرَّنَّكُم

بِٱللَّهِ ٱلۡغَرُورُ ۝ ﴾

*{O mankind! do your duty to your Lord, and fear
(the coming of) a Day when no father can avail*

95

---

aught for his son, nor a son avail aught for his father. Verily, the promise of Allah is true: let not then this present life deceive you, nor let the Chief Deceiver deceive you about Allah.[83]

May Allah make us and you successful towards what He loves and what pleases Him, and keep us from what He hates and prohibits. May He bless you and me concerning the mighty Quran. And may He benefit us and you with the verses and wise reminders. I end this speech and ask Allah to forgive you and me. Seek his forgiveness from him verily He is the Forgiver, the Merciful.

---

[83] Luqmaan: 33

Chapter Eleven: The Ruling on shaking hands with women who are not related to you

Muslim brother, be devoted to your religion and your female relatives concerning what has been requested of you (by your Lord). Muslim sister, by abstaining from what has been prohibited for you and by adhering to what has been commanded of you, you will please your Lord. Before you are several authentic narrations that will clarify the ruling of the prohibition of an evil custom that many ignorant people are involved in which is hand shaking between men and women. After these narratives, I relayed the text of a legal ruling given by al-'Allaamah, al-'Aalim, our Shaykh 'Abdul-'Azeez bin 'Abdillah bin Baaz, president of the Administration for Knowledge-based research, Legal Rulings, Missionary work, and Guidance.

The Narrations:

One - The noble female companion, Ameenah bint Raqeeqah said that when her and her friend went to give allegiance to the Messenger of Allah, peace be

---

upon him, they went to shake his hand, saying, "O Messenger of Allah, we have come to give allegiance to you." He said:

إِنِّي لاَ أُصَافِحُ النِّسَاءَ إِنَّمَا قَوْلِي لِمِائَةِ امْرَأَةٍ كَقَوْلِي لِامْرَأَةٍ وَاحِدَة

(I do not shake hands with women, instead my statement of acceptance for one hundred women is like my statement of acceptance for one woman.)[84]

And it has come in other chains of narrations that they said, "O Messenger of Allah, you do not shake hands with us?" And his response was the same.

Two – 'Aaishah bint as-Sideeq, may Allah be pleased with them both, said, "I swear by Allah that his, peace be upon him, hand never touched the hand of a woman during the allegiance. They would only give allegiance by his acceptance in word, 'I have accepted your allegiance by what you have stated.'"[85]

---

[84] Related by Maalik in *al-Muwattaa*, at-Tirmidhee, an-Nisaa'ee, and its chain of transmission is authentic.

[85] Related by al-Bukhaaree in his *Saheeh*.

Three - And 'Abdullah bin 'Amr, may Allah be pleased with them both said, "He did not take the allegiance of the women by shaking their hands."[86]

Four - And he, peace be upon him, said:

لِأَن يَطْعَن فِي رَأس رَجُلٍ بمخيْط مِنْ حَدِيْدٍ خَيْرٌ مِنْ أنْ يَمَسَّ امْرَأةً لا تحِلُّ لهُ

(I would rather be stabbed in the head with a needle of iron than to touch a woman that is not permissible for me.)[87]

The Text of the Question and the *Shaykh's* Legal Ruling:[88]

Question: It has become quite popular with us today when a man has been away from his country and then returns that the women from his group will come to him and greet him and kiss him. This is also

---

[86]Related by Ahmad and it was deemed good by as-Suyootee and al-Haythamee.

[87] Al-Mundhiree said in his book *at-Targheeb wa at-Tarheeb* that it was related by at-Tabaraanee and al-Bayhaqee and the narrators of al-Bayhaqee are all trustworthy.

[88] In the magazine of the Islamic University, 2nd Edition of Shawwaal 1390 A.H. It is the twelfth question pg. 49.

---

done during the two *Eeed* celebrations of *Eeed-ul-Fitr* and *Eeed-ul-Adhhaa*. Is this permissible?

Answer: It is known with the divinely legislated evidences derived from the Book and the *Sunnah* that a woman is not supposed to shake hands or kiss men she is not related to; whether this occurs during celebrations, upon the arrival from a journey, or any other reason. That is because the woman is a display of beauty and temptation. She is not to touch a man that is not her male relative. That can be her paternal male cousin or a distant relative (that is permissible for her to marry). She should not kiss them and they should not kiss her.

We do not know of any difference of opinion amongst the people of knowledge, may Allah have mercy upon them, concerning the prohibition of this issue or its rejection since it is from the causes of temptations and the means that Allah prohibited from leading to indecency and customs that oppose the Islamic legislation. The Muslims are not permitted to continue doing this and certainly not permitted to affiliate themselves with it. Rather, they must refrain from doing it and fight it. They must be grateful to Allah for blessing them with the

---

knowledge of His decree and He will grant them success in leaving off what He hates. Allah the Glorified sent the Messengers, peace be upon them, and at the head of them their leader and seal, our Prophet Muhammad, peace be upon him, to call the people to the oneness of Allah, to obey His commands, and to abandon His prohibitions while battling evil customs. It is obligatory to leave it and it is sufficient enough for them to just convey the salutations of peace, without touching or kissing. What Allah has legislated and allowed is more promising than what He has prohibited and dislikes. Likewise the greetings should be done while covered especially around teenage girls since uncovering the face is not permissible due to the great beauty displayed that Allah has prohibited from being shown. The Most High says:

﴿ وَلَا يُبْدِينَ زِينَتَهُنَّ إِلَّا لِبُعُولَتِهِنَّ أَوْ ءَابَآئِهِنَّ أَوْ ءَابَآءِ بُعُولَتِهِنَّ ۝ ﴾

_____

{...and not display their beauty except to their husbands, their fathers, their husbands' fathers...}[89]

And the Most High says:

﴿ وَإِذَا سَأَلْتُمُوهُنَّ مَتَـٰعًا فَسْـَٔلُوهُنَّ مِن وَرَآءِ حِجَابٍ ذَٰلِكُمْ أَطْهَرُ لِقُلُوبِكُمْ وَقُلُوبِهِنَّ ۚ ﴾

{And when ye ask (his ladies) for anything ye want ask them from before a screen: that makes for greater purity for your hearts and for theirs.}[90]

And the Most High says:

﴿ يَـٰٓأَيُّهَا ٱلنَّبِىُّ قُل لِّأَزْوَٰجِكَ وَبَنَاتِكَ وَنِسَآءِ ٱلْمُؤْمِنِينَ يُدْنِينَ عَلَيْهِنَّ مِن جَلَـٰبِيبِهِنَّ ۚ ذَٰلِكَ أَدْنَىٰٓ أَن يُعْرَفْنَ فَلَا يُؤْذَيْنَ ۗ وَكَانَ ٱللَّهُ غَفُورًا رَّحِيمًا ﴾

_____

[89] An-Noor: 31
[90] Al-Ahzaab: 53

{O Prophet! tell thy wives and daughters, and the believing women, that they should cast their outer garments over their persons (when abroad): that is most convenient, that they should be known (as such) and not molested. And Allah is Oft-Forgiving, Most Merciful.}[91]

And He says:

﴿ وَٱلْقَوَٰعِدُ مِنَ ٱلنِّسَآءِ ٱلَّتِى لَا يَرْجُونَ نِكَاحًا فَلَيْسَ

عَلَيْهِنَّ جُنَاحٌ أَن يَضَعْنَ ثِيَابَهُنَّ غَيْرَ مُتَبَرِّجَٰتٍۭ

بِزِينَةٍ ۖ وَأَن يَسْتَعْفِفْنَ خَيْرٌ لَّهُنَّ ۗ

وَٱللَّهُ سَمِيعٌ عَلِيمٌ ۝ ﴾

{Such elderly women as are past the prospect of marriage, there is no blame on them if they lay aside their (outer) garments, provided they make not a wanton display of their beauty: but it is best

---

[91] Al-Ahzaab: 59

---

for them to be modest: and Allah is One Who sees and knows all things.][92]

The elderly women are called *al-Qawaa'id* in this verse. Allah the Glorious explains that there is no harm if they pull their cover from their faces and the like if they are not done up with make-up, jewelry, henna, etc. Covering and wearing the head cover is better for them since it keeps away temptation. As for them having on make-up, jewelry, henna, etc then they should not lay aside their garments instead they should wear the head cover and cover up, even if they are elderly. It is known that the teenage girls must be covered in front of the men regardless of the circumstances, whether they are done up or not. That is because the temptation from them is far greater and the danger of them being uncovered is more immense. So if He has forbidden them from showing off their hair then the prohibition of touching and kissing is more deserving (to be left off). Touching and kissing are more serious than showing off the hair, both have results and effects that are sinful. It is obligatory to leave all of that, to warn from it, and to advise one another to abandon

---

[92] An-Noor: 60

_____

it. May Allah grant success to all in what He is pleased with as well as safety from the causes of His anger. Indeed He is generous and noble. And that which I advise all of you is to fear Allah, the Glorified and protect your practice of the religion. The most important and greatest is to protect the observance of the five prayers at their proper times and to perform them with humility and tranquility. Then men should rush to perform it with the congregation in the mosques, the places where the call to prayer is made and the name of Allah is mentioned, as He the Glorified says:

﴿ حَـٰفِظُوا۟ عَلَى ٱلصَّلَوَٰتِ وَٱلصَّلَوٰةِ ٱلۡوُسۡطَىٰ وَقُومُوا۟ لِلَّهِ

قَـٰنِتِينَ ۝ ﴾

{Guard strictly your (habit of) prayers, especially the Middle Prayer; and stand before Allah in a devout (frame of mind).}[93]

And the Most High says:

_____

[93] Al-Baqarah: 238

﴿ وَأَقِيمُوا۟ ٱلصَّلَوٰةَ وَءَاتُوا۟ ٱلزَّكَوٰةَ وَأَطِيعُوا۟ ٱلرَّسُولَ لَعَلَّكُمْ

تُرْحَمُونَ ۝ ﴾

{So establish regular Prayer and give regular Charity; and obey the Messenger; that ye may receive mercy.}[94]

And from the important issues is the issue of enjoining the good and forbidding the evil, cooperating on piety and righteousness, advising one another with the truth and with patience, all of this is the mannerisms of the believing men and women. Their descriptions are just as Allah has explained in His statement:

﴿ وَٱلْمُؤْمِنُونَ وَٱلْمُؤْمِنَتُ بَعْضُهُمْ أَوْلِيَآءُ بَعْضٍ يَأْمُرُونَ

بِٱلْمَعْرُوفِ وَيَنْهَوْنَ عَنِ ٱلْمُنكَرِ وَيُقِيمُونَ ٱلصَّلَوٰةَ

---

[94] An-Noor: 56

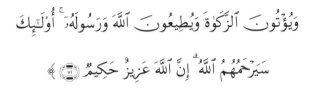

{The Believers, men and women, are protectors, one of another: they enjoin what is just, and forbid what is evil: they observe regular prayers, practice regular charity, and obey Allah and His Messenger. On them will Allah pour His Mercy: for Allah is Exalted in power, Wise.}[95]

I ask Allah, the Mighty and Majestic to grant us and all of you success to what He is pleased with, and that He guide us to His straight path. Indeed He is All-Hearing, the One who is near. Peace be upon you, and the mercy and blessings of Allah.

Your brother Faalih bin Naafi' al-Ma'dee

---

[95] At-Tawbah: 71

Chapter Twelve: The Prohibition of Women displaying their beauty and Intermingling with Men and the Issue surrounding *al-Hijaab*[96]

Muslims brothers and sisters, you should realize that the greatest of sins and the most harmful of tribulations occurring today is what is done by many women who go out of their homes, causing seduction and being the victims of seduction, going out displaying their beauty, jewelry, being perfumed, uncovered, displaying their attractiveness, and mixing with men. They displease Allah and inflict His anger and the descent of His punishment. Allah, the Mighty and Majestic says:

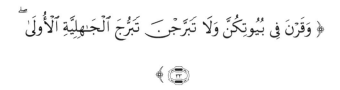

﴿ وَقَرْنَ فِى بُيُوتِكُنَّ وَلَا تَبَرَّجْنَ تَبَرُّجَ ٱلْجَٰهِلِيَّةِ ٱلْأُولَىٰ ﴾

﴿ ٣٣ ﴾

---

[96] Written by: *ash-Shaykh* 'Abdur-Rahmaan al-Hammaad al-'Umar

---

{And stay in your houses, and do not display yourselves like that of the times of ignorance.}

And the Glorified and Most High says:

﴿ وَلَا يُبْدِينَ زِينَتَهُنَّ ۖ ۝ ﴾

{That they should not display their beauty and ornaments...}[97]

And the Prophet, peace be upon him, said:

صَنَفَان مِنْ أهْل النَّار لَمْ أرَهمَا : قَوْمٌ مَعَهُمْ سِيَاطٌ كَأذْنَابِ البَقَرِ يَضْرِبُوْنَ بهَا النَّاسَ وَ نِسَاءٌ كَاسِيَاتٌ عَارِيَاتٌ مُمِيْلَاتٌ مَائِلَاتٌ رُءُوسُهُنَّ كَأسْنِمَةِ البُخْتِ المَائِلَةِ لاَ يَدْخُلْنَ الجَنَّةَ وَ لاَ يَجِدْنَ رِيْحَهَا وَ إن رِيْحهَا لَيُوجَد مِنْ مَسِيْرةِ كَذَا وَ كَذَا

(There were two types of people from the inhabitants of the Hellfire that I had never seen before. The first was a group of people with whips like the tails of cows in which they struck the people with. The second were women clothed yet naked, misguided while leading others astray, their heads were like the humps of the long necked camels leaning to one

---

[97] An-Noor: 30

side. They will not enter paradise nor will they smell
its fragrance. If they would have smelled it the
presence of its distance would be like this and like
this.)[98]

His statement, "I had never seen before" means
during his lifetime. This narration is from his
miracles as this has occurred exactly as he, peace be
upon him, stated it would. Today you find the
women covered but because of their short skirts they
are naked from their body parts that are showing.
You find the women covered, they have clothes on
but their head covering is see through and doesn't
cover them, so they are naked because their body
parts are showing from behind their clothes (and
head covering). She appears to be naked. But
perhaps the most far reaching temptation is tight
clothes that show the woman's entire shape and her
attractiveness. It is the most popular type of clothes
used by prostitutes, the Western non-Muslim
women, and others who imitate them from those
women who ascribe themselves to Islam.
The meaning of the word مُمِيْلاَتٌ Mumeelaat here
means they expose others to their wrong deeds. And

---

[98] Related by Muslim.

قَضَايَا تَهُمُّ المَرْأَةُ

Issues the Muslim Woman Should Concern Herself With

_____

it is said that مَائِلَاتٌ Maailaat are women who style
their hair in this manner which is the style of the
prostitutes. And the مُمِيْلَاتٌ Mumeelaat are the ones
who style others hair in the same manner as it is the
case for many women today who do the hair of their
head above the top or front part. We seek refuge in
Allah from the evil of tribulations that have
appeared and those that still haven't manifested.

So fear Allah woman, you who openly displays your
beauty in front of the people. Fear Allah, you who
goes out to the markets uncovered. Fear Allah, you
who mixes with men, checking them out and letting
them check you out. Fear Allah woman, if you
believe in Allah and in standing before Him,
knowing that these actions are prohibited for you to
do. Fear Allah, you who ride alone with a driver or
goes to a male doctor or anyone else without having
one of your male relative escorts with you. Fear
Allah, you who goes out uncovered, wearing no head
cover, indeed uncovered hair causes temptation and
evil. It opposes the command of Allah and His
Messenger, peace be upon him. Fear Allah Muslim
woman, repent to Him if you are doing any of these
sinful deeds. By Allah, His punishment is severe.
Fear Allah, you who expose women and stare at

_____

them lustfully. This is prohibited and is a sin. It is not permissible. Allah Most High says:

$$ ﴿ قُل لِّلْمُؤْمِنِينَ يَغُضُّوا۟ مِنْ أَبْصَـٰرِهِمْ وَيَحْفَظُوا۟ فُرُوجَهُمْ ۚ ذَٰلِكَ أَزْكَىٰ لَهُمْ ۗ إِنَّ ٱللَّهَ خَبِيرُۢ بِمَا يَصْنَعُونَ ٣٠ ﴾ $$

{Say to the believing men that they should lower their gaze and guard their modesty: that will make for greater purity for them: and Allah is well acquainted with all that they do.}[99]

Fear Allah, you who leave your women and daughters upon one of the many conditions that have been mentioned in addition to others that Allah has prohibited. Make them cover (their bodies), observe the proper head covering, preserve their modesty, and remain in their homes. Save yourselves and your family from the fire whose fuel is men and stones. You are the responsible shepherds over your flocks and with Allah is success.

_____

[99] An-Noor: 30

Chapter Thirteen: From the Rulings on Menstruation, Continuous Vaginal Bleeding, and Post-Natal Bleeding

From Saalih bin Ahmad al-Khuraysee to our brothers, the Imams of the mosques who will read this, may Allah grant us and all of you success to the path of righteousness and guidance. May He keep us and you from the path of sin and destruction. May the peace, mercy, and blessings of Allah be upon you. To proceed:

This is a suitable time to bring to attention and remind all of you of some of what Allah the Glorified has obligated us and all of you with, from the religious obligations and Islamic duties and rights of faith. And because this is a general gathering set up for both the men and the women. This is the arrival of a blessed month in which Allah makes (life) a race course for those who will compete (in doing good deeds) and it is a magnificent time of the year for the world. The Most High says, and He is the most truthful of those who speak:

{But teach (thy Message): for teaching benefits the Believers.}[100]

It is imperative that every Imam, that is responsible for running a mosque, benefit his congregation of men and women and direct them to righteousness and well being for both their livelihood and for their hereafter. Indeed this is cooperation on piety and God-consciousness as well as helping one another to observe truth and patience. From the most important issues and obligations is the observance of the five prayers. The Imam must encourage (its performance) and command (the men) to observe it in congregation. He goes out to visit those who fail to pray in congregation. The Imam is responsible for this so it is incumbent that he conveys what he is able to (about the prayer) and explains its great virtue and everything else affiliated with prayer. He explains its pillars, its obligations and its conditions. He explains the necessary parts of ablution, its conditions and its nullifiers. Then he explains the

---

[100] Adh-Dhaariyaat: 55

---

alms and its status in the divine legislation and that it is one of the pillars of Islam and its fundamentals. Then he explains what he is able to concerning fasting and that the fast in the month of Ramadan is one of the pillars of Islam. He explains the obligations, what is recommended, and the things that the fasting person is forbidden from doing, along with striving with one's ability to do what is disliked (while fasting).

Likewise he should encourage his congregation to hasten in doing good deeds and to be mindful of time before it passes because it is a time that Allah has designated above any other time. The good in this time is worth one thousand good deeds, and the actions in it are doubled.

Focus should also be placed on issues specific to women, issues such as menstruation, abnormal bleeding, and post natal bleeding. (She should know) the difference between (these three things) and what is considered valid menstrual bleeding when its normal routine is interrupted. So if the woman's cycle is abnormal she knows by using good judgment, at times the blood is black, thick and having a bad odor and at times it is red, thin and

----

odorless. So if there is a time that her menstruation is black, thick and smells and that is not its normal condition then it is known as al-Istihaadhah. Al-Istihaadhah is the flow of blood that appears from its usual time. If the blood comes to her in this manner, then she performs the regular acts of worship such as fasting, prayer, reading Quran, etc. She isn't exempt (from worship). If her cycle is broken and it's not distinct she is to sit for her menses six or seven days every month, then she resumes praying and fasting.

As for the menstruating woman, then there are rulings for her (to know): From these rulings is if she gets her menses once the time of prayer enters, she makes up this prayer time when she completes her menstruation.

From these rulings (of menstruation for her to understand) is if her menstruation is over before the sun sets then she prays adh-Dhuhr (the noon prayer) and al-'Asr (the afternoon prayer) and if her menstruation is over before the time of al-Fajr (morning prayer) then she prays al-Maghrib (sunset

116

---

prayer) and *al-'Ishaa* (night prayer)[101]. If her menstruation is over before sunrise then she only prays *al-Fajr*.

From these rulings (of menstruation for her to understand) is if her menstruation is over before the coming of *al-Fajr* then she eats a light breakfast known as (*as-Suhoor*) and makes the intention to fast. If she doesn't bathe until after the rising of the sun then her fast is still valid.

From these rulings (of menstruation for her to understand) is if she feels the flow of blood before the setting of the sun she completes the day even if the blood doesn't flow after its setting.[102] And

---

[101] *Shaykh* Muhammad as-Saalih al-'Uthaymeen says in his treatise *ad-Dimaa at-Tabee'ah li-Nisaa* (Natural Blood of the Women), page 24, 2nd Edition, "The correct stance is that it is not obligatory for her unless she is aware of the time which is only *al-'Asr* and the later part of *al-'Ishaa* based on the statement of the Prophet, peace be upon him: (Whoever catches the last *Rak'ah* of *al-'Asr* before the setting of the sun, has caught *al-'Asr*.)
[102] Shaykh Ibn 'Uthaymeen says in the previous source, page 28, "If she feels the flow of menstruation before the setting of the sun but nothing comes down until after the setting of the sun then her fast is complete and not invalidated according to the correct stance. That is because the blood that is in the upper part of her has no ruling applied to it and because the Prophet, peace be upon him, ordered to bathe with the expulsion of

included in these rulings is that if her menstruation is over at its normal time and she fasted then the blood returned, her fast is still valid and it is not required for her to make it up. For example, if her normal menstruation is for eight days but she only sees blood for four days, then she sees it completely clean on the fifth or sixth day then she must fast these two days. If the blood returns to her on the seventh and eighth day it doesn't affect her, her fast on the fifth and sixth day is valid. However the complete state of cleanliness is (verified) by her checking for whiteness that she sees if she were to put cotton in the area (of menstruation) and it doesn't change (color).

As for the woman who has post partum bleeding, then it depends on when she saw the blood. Did she see it after the delivery, the day before, or was it two days with marks of blood? Therefore she leaves off all acts of worship and anything before the delivery is deemed as an-Nifaas (post partum bleeding) if there were any signs such as severe pain, etc. When she purifies herself ten days, more or less after the birth, she must not purify herself or perform acts of

---

seminal fluid not due to its flow, so therefore menstruation takes the same ruling."

---

worship such as fasting, prayer, or anything else. She doesn't have to make them back up. If the blood returns to her within forty days then it's still deemed as post partum bleeding and she leaves off worship. As for her fast before the post-partum bleeding, then it is valid. She doesn't have to make it up. If the blood returns after forty days and it coincides with the normal menstrual cycle then it is considered menstruation. If it doesn't coincide with the normal menstrual cycle then it is bad blood, she prays and fast and she doesn't have to make it up.

The bath taken after menstruation and post partum bleeding is obligatory upon every woman if the bleeding was interrupted suddenly and it coincides with the time of prayer. As for the woman experiencing abnormal bleeding then the ruling concerning her condition has been explained previously. However she must perform ablution for every prayer and it is recommended for her to bathe for every prayer. It is permissible for her to combine two prayers by delaying *adh-Dhuhr* and praying *al-'Asr* early, and combine and delay *al-Maghrib* and pray *al-'Ishaa* early. She is combining her prayers due to hardship.

If the blood increases then she is to plug up that area (of bleeding) during the time of prayer and she can pray. If blood is apparent then she doesn't pay attention to it based on the statement of the Prophet, peace be upon him:

وَ إِنْ قَطَرَ الدَّمُ عَلَى الحَصِيرِ

(...Even if blood were to drop on the mat (that the woman is praying on).)[103]

And her prayer is considered valid. Likewise the woman who is pregnant and sees blood then her ruling is like the ruling of the woman who experiences abnormal bleeding when it comes to acts of worship; she fasts and prays and she doesn't have to make it up.[104] The woman that is pregnant with a fetus at its earliest stage, if she is sure that she didn't abort it then she continues performing acts of worship. However, if anything comes down and it is

---

[103] Related by Ahmad and Ibn Maajah.

[104] *Shaykh* Ibn 'Uthaymeen says in the same book on page 15, "The correct stance is that flowing blood of a pregnant woman is menstruation as long as there is no reason that alters its consideration as menstruation blood. To this effect, there is nothing in the Book or *Sunnah* that indicates that a pregnant woman may not have menstruation."

---

evident that it is the fetus then her ruling is the ruling of the woman who is experiencing post partum bleeding. She leaves off all acts of worship, and if it wasn't the fetus then her ruling is that of a woman experiencing abnormal bleeding, she fasts, prays and performs acts of worship.

It is necessary for all men and women to fear Allah the Mighty and Glorious, privately and publicly, and for them to be chaste and to lower their gaze. Indeed adultery of the eyes starts with the look, as it is relayed in the prophetic narration. The look is a poisonous arrow from the arrows of *Iblees*.

Just as it is obligatory for the women not to display their beauty such as their clothes underneath and the like, except to those mentioned in the noble verse contained within the statement of the Most High:

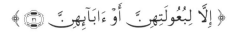

{...Except to their husbands or their fathers...}[105]

---

[105] An-Noor: 31

And everyone else included in this verse. As for her showing off the attractive clothing underneath her garment in the markets along with displaying her rings and other jewelry while going out perfumed, then this is impermissible. It is considered an act of publicly displaying beauty that was practiced in the days of Ignorance, before the advent of Islam. This is a practice that Allah the Glorified and Most High prohibited and found fault with contained within the commandment of His great Book. And if the woman goes out perfumed in this condition (of exposing herself) then this is an even greater sin as it relayed in the prophetic narration:

إِذَا خَرَجَتِ المَرْأَةُ مُتَطَيِّبَة فَهِيَ زَانِية

(When the woman goes out perfumed she is adulterous.)[106]

This means that she engages in the sin of adultery. Now if goes out without permission of her husband then it is an even greater sin based on the prophetic narration:

----

[106] Related by Aboo Daawud and at-Tirmidhee who said that it was *Hasan Saheeh* (A good and authentic narration).

إِذَا خَرَجَتِ الْمَرْأَةُ بِغَيْرِ إِذْنِ زَوْجِهَا لَعَنَتْهَا الْمَلَائِكَةُ حَتَّى تَرْجِعَ

(When the woman goes out without her husband's permission, the angels curse her until she returns.)[107]

The woman cannot get any closer to Allah than staying in her home like in the prophetic narration:

الْمَرْأَةُ عَوْرَة فَاحْبِسُوهَا فِي الْبُيُوتِ فَإِن الْمَرْأَة إِذَا خَرَجَتْ مِنْ بَيْتِهَا اسْتَشْرَفَهَا الشَّيْطَانُ

(The woman is 'Awrah, so keep her in the home. Indeed the woman, when she goes out of her house Shaytaan accompanies her.)[108]

A woman doesn't seek the pleasure of Allah like when she sits in her house and worships her Lord and obeys her husband. 'Ali, may Allah be pleased with him, said to his wife, may Allah be pleased with her, "Faatimah, what is the best thing a woman can do?" She said, "That she doesn't see men, and that men do not see her."[109] And he said, may Allah be pleased with him, "Are you not shy or jealous to

---

[107] Related by at-Tabaraanee.
[108] Imam adh-Dhahabee mentioned it in al-Kabaair, page 170.
[109] Imam adh-Dhahabee mentioned it in al-Kabaair, page 170.

---

allow your wife to go out amongst men, her looking at them and them looking at her?" So it is befitting for the woman who fears Allah the Mighty and Glorious to strive in obeying Allah and His Messenger and her husband. That she seeks His pleasure and strives for it as in the narration:

إِذَا صَلَّتِ المَرْأَةُ خَمْسَهَا وَ صَامَتْ شَهْرَهَا وَ أَطَاعَتْ بعْلَهَا فَلْتَدْخُلْ مِنْ أَيِّ أَبْوَابِ الجَنَّةِ شَاءَتْ

(If a woman prays the five daily prayers, fasts in *Ramadhaan*, and obeys her husband, then she can enter paradise from any door she wants.)

Therefore it is binding on the husbands to take control of their women and command them not to go out improperly covered because the husband is a shepherd over the members of his home and he will be asked about his flock.

If the woman is commanded to obey her husband and to seek his pleasure then the husband is also commanded to be good to her and to be generous with her and grant her, her rights such as money, clothes, and living with them in kindness based on the statement of the Most High:

﴿ وَعَاشِرُوهُنَّ بِٱلْمَعْرُوفِ ۝ ﴾

{Live with them on a footing of kindness and equity.}[110]

And based on the statement of the Prophet, peace be upon him:

إِسْتَوْصُوا بِالنِّسَاءِ خَيْرًا فَإِنَّهُنَّ عَوَانٍ عِنْدَكُمْ أَخَذْتُمُوهُنَّ بِأَمَانَةِ اللهِ وَ اسْتَحْلَلْتُمْ فُرُوجَهُنَّ بِكَلِمَةِ اللهِ

(Treat your women kindly for they are in your care, you took them as a trust from Allah and they were made permissible for you by the word of Allah...)[111]

It is a duty of the wife, that when her husband calls her that she responds to him even if she was sitting atop of the camel's hump. If she does not go to him and he spends the night angry with her then the angels curse her until she wakes up.[112] And it has been relayed from the Prophet, peace be upon him, that he said in a sermon on the *Eeed* prayer:

---

[110] An-Nisaa'a: 19

[111] Related by Ibn Maajah and at-Tirmidhee who said it was a narration that was good and authentic.

[112] As it is found in the narration relayed by al-Bukhaaree, Muslim, and others.

يَا مَعْشَرَ النِّسَاءِ تَصَدَّقْنَ وَ لَوْ مِنْ حُلِيِّكُنَّ فَإِنَّكُنَّ أَكْثَرُ حَطَبِ جَهَنَّم

(Assembly of women! Give charity even if it is from your jewelry, for most of you will be firewood for the hellfire.)

A woman stood up and asked, "Why Messenger of Allah?" He said:

لِأَنَّكُنَّ تَكْثُرْنَ الشِّكَايَةَ وَ تَكْفُرْنَ الْعَشِيرَ

(Because you constantly complain and are ungrateful to your husbands.)

And in another narration:

وَ تَكْثُرْنَ اللَّعْنَ لَوْ أَحْسَنت عَلَى إِحْدَاهُنَّ الدَّهْرَ ثُمَّ رَأَتْ شَيْئًا قَالَتْ مَا رَأَيْتُ مِنْكَ خَيْرًا قَط

(And you constantly curse your husband's even if they are good to you all of the time and you see anything objectionable you say, "I have never seen any good in him.")[113]

---

[113] Related by Muslim and others.

It is a duty for all of the men and women to repent to Allah from these acts and others. Allah associates success, happiness, and victory together in His statement:

﴿ قُل لِّلْمُؤْمِنِينَ يَغُضُّوا مِنْ أَبْصَـٰرِهِمْ وَيَحْفَظُوا فُرُوجَهُمْ ۩ ﴾

{Say to the believing men that they should lower their gaze and guard their modesty.}[114]

Up to His statement:

﴿ وَقُل لِّلْمُؤْمِنَـٰتِ يَغْضُضْنَ مِنْ أَبْصَـٰرِهِنَّ وَيَحْفَظْنَ فُرُوجَهُنَّ ۩ ﴾

{...And say to the believing women that they should lower their gaze and guard their modesty.}

Then He ends the verse saying:

----

[114] An-Noor: 30

127

﴿ وَتُوبُوٓاْ إِلَى ٱللَّهِ جَمِيعًا أَيُّهَ ٱلْمُؤْمِنُونَ لَعَلَّكُمْ

تُفْلِحُونَ ۝ ﴾

*[...And O ye Believers! Repent towards Allah, that
ye may attain Bliss.]*[115]

But the issue of sincere and pure repentance derives
from three conditions: the first is to be regretful of
what has been done, the second is abstinence from
the bad deeds that the person committed, the third
is firm resolve not to commit the sin again. This is
the repentance that was mentioned in the previous
verse. The one who repents in this manner is like
one who did not commit any sin and he obtains
happiness and success in this life and in the
hereafter. As for the one who repents with his
tongue but persists upon sin and continues with acts
of sins that anger Allah, then this type of repentance
is not useful or beneficial. Therefore it is obligatory
for you Muslim brothers to convey this advice to
your congregations and repeat it and add whatever
good can be contributed to it so that the real intent
is conveyed. This is the way of the Messengers and

---

[115] An-Noor: 31

---

those who followed them. And you know the gain and reward that results from that, as the Prophet, peace be upon him, said to 'Ali, may Allah be pleased with him:

فَوَاللهِ لأَنْ يَهْدِيَ اللهُ بِكَ رَجُلاً وَاحِدًا خَيْرٌ لَكَ مِنْ حُمْرِ النَّعَم

(By Allah, that one person is guided because of you is better for you than (possessing) the red camels.)[116]

The causes of good and evil found here are not restricted to this article alone, this is just a position of enlightenment. The sensible intellectual suffices with less than that while the question at hand falls upon everyone. Every Imam is responsible before Allah for his congregation. So fear Allah and consider the (proper) response for the question (that you will be questioned for) and the correct stance for the response. Allah is the responsible one, the one who we hope will respond (to our request) that He bless us and all of you with the acceptance (of our fasts and good deeds) in this blessed month. And that He makes us and you from those who win the prize of the noble Lord which no other prizes can be

---

[116] Related by al-Bukhaaree and Muslim.

---

compared to. Indeed He is noble and generous. And may the prayers of Allah be upon Muhammad, his family, and companions and peace.

Chapter Fourteen: Regarding the Rulings where Women obtain half of what Men are given in Perspective

One – Inheritance, the Most High says:

﴿ يُوصِيكُمُ ٱللَّهُ فِىٓ أَوْلَٰدِكُمْ ۖ لِلذَّكَرِ مِثْلُ حَظِّ

ٱلْأُنثَيَيْنِ ۚ ⑪ ﴾

{Allah (thus) directs you as regards your children's (inheritance): to the male, a portion equal to that of two females.}[117]

Two – Blood money, the reparation of the free Muslim woman is half of the blood money of the free Muslim man. Ibn Mundhir and Ibn 'Abdil-Barr said that the people of knowledge are unanimous that the blood money of the woman is half that of the man.[118]

Three – The 'Aqeeqah Ceremony, which is to slaughter two goats upon the birth of a boy and one

---

[117] An-Nisaa'a: 11
[118] Related by at-Tirmidhee and he authenticated it.

_____

goat on the birth of a girl. It has been narrated by
'Aaishah, may Allah be pleased with her, that she
said that the Prophet, peace be upon him, ordered
them to slaughter two goats of the same kind for a
boy and one for a girl.[119] The meaning of 'being of
the same kind' here means the age of the animal so
that they are of equal measure when distributed after
slaughtering.

Four – In giving Testimony, Allah the Most High
says:

﴿ وَٱسْتَشْهِدُوا۟ شَهِيدَيْنِ مِن رِّجَالِكُمْ ۖ فَإِن لَّمْ يَكُونَا

رَجُلَيْنِ فَرَجُلٌ وَٱمْرَأَتَانِ مِمَّن تَرْضَوْنَ مِنَ ٱلشُّهَدَآءِ أَن

تَضِلَّ إِحْدَىٰهُمَا فَتُذَكِّرَ إِحْدَىٰهُمَا ٱلْأُخْرَىٰ ۚ ﴿٢٨٢﴾ ﴾

{And get two witnesses, out of your own men, and
if there are not two men, then a man and two
women, such as ye choose, for witnesses, so that if
one of them errs, the other can remind her.}[120]

_____

[119] In *al-Mughnee* and *ash-Sharh al-Kabeer* (10/131).
[120] Al-Baqarah: 282

132

Five – Emancipation, which is to free a slave and wipe his debt clean. It has been authentically reported from Aboo Hurayrah, may Allah be pleased with him, that he said that the Messenger of Allah, peace be upon him said:

أَيُّمَا امْرِئٍ مُسْلِمٍ أَعْتَقَ امْرَأً مُسْلِمًا اسْتَنْقَذَ اللَّهُ بِكُلِّ عُضْوٍ مِنْهُ عُضْوًا مِنْهُ مِنْ النَّارِ

(Any Muslim who frees a Muslim slave will have Allah save every part of his body from the hellfire.)[121]

And from Aboo Umaamah, may Allah be pleased with him, that the Prophet, peace be upon him, said:

وَ أَيُّمَا امْرِئٍ مُسْلِمٍ أَعْتَقَ امْرَأَتَيْنِ مُسْلِمَتَيْنِ كَانَتَا فِكَاكُهُ مِنَ النَّارِ

(Any Muslim who frees two female Muslim slaves will be freed from the hellfire.)[122]

Six – Inheritance is a gift put in place for the benefit of the children. What has been legislated is that the male receives the portion of two females.

---

[121] It is agreed upon.
[122] Related by at-Tirmidhee and he authenticated it.

Seven – Prayer, the woman is absolved of praying on the days of menstruation. The most according to some scholars is fifteen days which is half a month. The correct view is that there is no set limit to indicate the days where menstruation can be less or when it can be more. This has been the choice of *Shaykh-ul-Islaam*, Ibn Taymiyyah and a group of scholars.[123]

---

[123] Reference Ibn Rajab's *al-Qawaaid*, 322, principle 148.

Chapter Fifteen: Critiquing Equality of the Sexes in Light of Islam[124]

Amongst us today are many people who believe that women and men are equal. They believe that what is obligatory for women is obligatory for men and what is imposed upon women is imposed upon men. They believe that when it comes to the divine rulings that there is no difference between the two types since women are the sister relatives of men. And they don't stop there, they begin supporting this view until they fanatically side with it, putting down the opinion of whoever opposes them from the people of Islam as if the people do not understand the commands of Islam. Not one ruling from the divine rulings reaches their ears. So the Islamic religion is one way and those who ascribe to (equality of the sexes) are another. There is no doubt that this opinion is a filthy one, far from the proven evidences of the Book and the *Sunnah*. Just listen to the evidences from the Book and the *Sunnah* concerning some of the distinct differences between men and

---

[124] From the *ar-Rasaail al-Hassaan fee Nasaaih-il-Ikhwaan* by ash-Shaykh 'Abdullah bin Muhammad bin Hameed, may Allah have mercy upon him, pg. 20-22.

women and the comparison of the first type over the second.

One – Allah the Most High says:

﴿ ٱلرِّجَالُ قَوَّٰمُونَ عَلَى ٱلنِّسَآءِ بِمَا فَضَّلَ ٱللَّهُ بَعْضَهُمْ عَلَىٰ بَعْضٍ وَبِمَآ أَنفَقُوا۟ مِنْ أَمْوَٰلِهِمْ ۚ ۖ ٣٤ ﴾

{Men are the protectors and maintainers of women, because Allah has given the one more (strength) than the other, and because they support them from their means.}[125]

This verse clearly indicates that the man is responsible for maintaining the woman and in protecting and taking care of her. The man has a strong frame of mind, his own complete and natural characteristics. He possesses a strong mind, the soundness of his perception concerning the basics of issues and their purposes, in addition to his ability to earn and spend on everything. Therefore men are responsible for spending on the women and in

---

[125] An-Nisaa'a: 34

136

---

establishing the leadership of the home while the woman is to maintain her natural position which is pregnancy, childbirth, and in raising the children. She is honorable concerning her flock and content, not worried about her maintenance or the maintenance of her children.

Two – Allah the Most High says:

﴿ فَٱنكِحُواْ مَا طَابَ لَكُم مِّنَ ٱلنِّسَآءِ مَثْنَىٰ وَثُلَٰثَ وَرُبَٰعَ ۖ ٣ ﴾

{Marry women of your choice, two, or three, or four.}[126]

This verse clarifies that Allah, the Glorified, the Most High has allowed the man to take four wives when he knows within himself that he can be just amongst them. It is not permissible for the woman to marry more than one man because this will mix the lineages and cause many troubles. The woman cannot fulfill the desires of many men all at once as well as not being able to maintain order in the

---

[126] An-Nisaa'a: 3

---

homes and direct the families. Therefore, how after all of this has been pointed out can it be said that women are equal to men?

Three – Allah the Most High says:

﴿ يُوصِيكُمُ ٱللَّهُ فِىٓ أَوْلَٰدِكُمْ ۖ لِلذَّكَرِ مِثْلُ حَظِّ ٱلْأُنثَيَيْنِ ۚ ۝ ﴾

{Allah (thus) directs you as regards your children's (inheritance): to the male, a portion equal to that of two females.}[127]

And His statement:

﴿ وَإِن كَانُوٓاْ إِخْوَةً رِّجَالًا وَنِسَآءً فَلِلذَّكَرِ مِثْلُ حَظِّ ٱلْأُنثَيَيْنِ ۚ ۝ ﴾

{If there are brothers and sisters, (they share), the male having twice the share of the female.}[128]

---

[127] An-Nisaa'a: 11
[128] An-Nisaa'a: 176

These two verses clarify that the male is left an inheritance equal to two females from amongst his sisters. The wisdom behind that, and Allah knows best, is that there will be a time when the man will marry and he will have children and need to spend on them and his wife. It will be requested of him at times to have visitors in his home (to be guest to and to serve). It is the opposite for the female. There will be a time when she will be paired with a suitable man who will marry her and maintain her affairs, spending on food, drink, clothes, and a place to live for her and her children. She won't spend one Halalah[129] from her own wealth, one wouldn't dream of making her home his haven (at her exclusion) since that incites suspicions and causes doubts and uncertainties, so how can it be said that women are equal to men under these circumstances?

Four - Allah the Most High says:

---

[129] **T.N:** A Halalah is from the currency of Saudi Arabia. One hundred Halalah equals one Saudi Riyal.

﴿ وَٱسْتَشْهِدُوا۟ شَهِيدَيْنِ مِن رِّجَالِكُمْ ۖ فَإِن لَّمْ يَكُونَا رَجُلَيْنِ فَرَجُلٌ وَٱمْرَأَتَانِ مِمَّن تَرْضَوْنَ مِنَ ٱلشُّهَدَآءِ ﴾ ۝

{And get two witnesses, out of your own men, and if there are not two men, then a man and two women, such as ye choose, for witnesses.}[130]

This noble verse proves that when it comes to the witness testimony and there are two men to give testimony then it makes the transaction more complete, stronger, and more accurate. If only one man is available then the witness of two women suffices in place of the other male witness. This is due to the weakness of the woman's memory and the incompleteness of her preciseness. The man is stronger intelligent wise than the woman as the verse indicates and just as the unbiased evidence supports him, bearing witness that he possesses deeply-rooted understanding. Many of the rulings do not accept the witness of the women like the legal punishments, retributions, etc., so how can it be said that women are equal to men?

---

[130] Al-Baqarah: 282

Five – And from the *Sunnah*, what has been relayed by al-Bukhaaree and others from the statement of the Prophet, peace be upon him, in the narrative:

مَا رَأَيْتُ مِنْ نَاقِصَاتِ عَقْلٍ وَ دِيْنٍ أَذْهَبَ لِلُبِّ الرَّجُلِ الحَازِم مِنْ إِحْدَاكُنَّ

(I have not seen anyone more deficient in intelligence and religion than you. A cautious sensible man could be led astray by some of you.)[131]

This is an explicit text regarding the deficiency of the woman's intelligence and religion in comparison to the man based on the stipulation that the one who prays a portion of one's life is not equal to the one who prays all of one's life. And one who fasts the month of Ramadan from beginning to end is not equal to the one who only fasts a portion of it. Just as one is not equal in giving the testimony of a man because of the completeness of his intelligence and the strength of his accuracy as opposed to the one whose testimony is half the testimony (of a male) due to the weakness of her intelligence and incompleteness of her accurateness. So whoever

---

[131] Related by al-Bukhaaree.

---

establishes equality between man and woman has harmed Islam and traverses the path of deviance.

Six – And what was related by Ahmad, al-Bukhaaree, and others from the narration of Aboo Bakr, may Allah be pleased with him, regarding what destroyed the ruler of Persia, the Prophet, peace be upon him, said:

مَن اسْتَخْلَفَتْ فَارس عَلَيْهَا؟ قَالُوا : إِبْنَته قَالَ : لَنْ يُفْلِحَ قَوْمٌ وَلُوا
أَمْرَهُمْ إِمْرَأَةً

("Who has the ruler of Persia left to succeed him?" They said, "His daughter." He responded, peace be upon him, "Prosperity will never be obtained by a people who appoint a woman over their affairs.")

This narration stipulates that it is not permissible for a woman to hold the position of rulership and that prosperity will be obliterated since the people appointed a woman over themselves as a leader. Whenever prosperity is void then disappointment and failure soon follow. Therefore it is clarified that this important position is reserved for men. The people of knowledge have explicitly explained that it is not permissible for the woman to be appointed as

---

a ruler and that she is not to be a judge, an Imam in prayer, one who calls the men to prayer, and not a preacher of the Friday sermon. And due to this a poet once took this meaning and wrote, "It is not for the women to write, to lead prayers, and give the Friday sermons. This is (reserved for us, men) and they have the right for us to spend the night with them and to have relations with them."

Seven – What has been relayed by the two *Shaykhs* and others that the Prophet, peace be upon him, said:

لاَ يَخْلُوَنَّ رَجُلٌ بِامْرَأَةٍ إلاَّ وَ مَعَهَا ذُو مَحْرَمٍ

(A man does not seclude himself with a woman unless there is a male relative escort with her.)

This narration proves that it is prohibited for a man to be alone with a woman unless there is a male relative escort with her such as her husband or someone else. As for the man being alone with another man, then there is no fear of anything occurring. That is because there is no indication that the meaning is on account of the man being inclined to another man as opposed to the woman. The man is not safe from (feeling for) her due to the strong needs (of desire that exists) from both as in the last narrative:

$$ لَا يَخْلُونَ رَجُلٌ بِامْرَأَةٍ فَـإِنَّ الشَّيْطَانَ ثَالِثُهُمَا $$

(A man and a woman do not seclude themselves except that *Shaytaan* is the third amongst them.)[132]

So how can it be said that there is equality between a man and a woman? This is propaganda or doubt that the enemies of Islam have established to the point that they become serious and their danger increases. Many whose hearts have been covered in darkness and who will not smell the fragrance of faith call to (these propaganda ideas and doubts), than those who ascribe to the Islamic religion.

Eight – What has been related by Ahmad, al-Bukhaaree, Muslim, and others that the Prophet, peace be upon him, said:

$$ لَا يُحِلُّ لِإِمْرَأَةٍ أَنْ تَصُوْمَ وَ زَوْجُهَا حَاضِرٌ إلاَّ بِإِذْنِهِ $$

---

[132] Related by Ahmad and at-Tirmidhee, and al-Haakim authenticated it.

(It is not permissible for the woman to fast while her husband is present unless by his permission.)

This means that it is not permissible for the woman to fast voluntarily while her husband is home unless he allows her to. That is because her fast is not obligatory while her obedience to him is obligatory for her. Therefore her fast will be considered as a crime committed out of disobedience and with no reward.

Nine – And it has come in the narration of Mu'aadh, may Allah be pleased with him, that the Messenger of Allah, peace be upon him, said:

دِيَةُ المَرْأَةِ نِصْفُ دِيَةِ الرَّجُلِ

(The blood money of the woman is half of the blood money of the man.)[133]

And it is unanimously agreed upon by the scholars. This clarifies the false statement previously mentioned of those who say that women are equal to men concerning all of the divine rulings. This is a

---

[133] It was declared weak by al-Albaanee and it has its evidences in which acting according to it is a unanimous decision.

---

vile allegation that opposes the Book and the *Sunnah*. Each of its corruptions is known within simple reasoning. The prophetic texts prove the differences between women and men and that they are not equal. There are many such as the narration:

التَّسْبِيْحُ لِلرِّجَالِ وَ التَّصْفِيْقُ لِلنِّسَاءِ

(Saying the *Tasbeeh* is for the men and clapping is for the women.)[134]

And the narration:

لَيْسَ عَلَى النِّسَاءِ حَلْقٌ وَ إِنَّمَا يَقْصِرْنَ

(It is not obligatory for the woman to shave her head but instead just to cut a portion of it off.)[135]

And the narration:

لَوْ كُنْتُ آمِرًا أَحَدًا أَنْ يَسْجُدَ لِأَحَدٍ لَأَمَرْتُ المَرْأَةَ أَنْ تَسْجُدَ لِزَوْجِهَا

---

[134] Related by al-Bukhaaree and Muslims as well as others.
[135] Related by Aboo Daawud and ad-Daarqutnee in the section on *Hajj* and ‘*Umrah*.

(If I were to command anyone to prostrate to another, I would command the women to prostrate to her husband.)[136]

And the narration:

عَلَيْكُنَّ بِحَافاتِ الطَّرِيْق

(Stay on the sides of the road.)[137]

And the narration:

لاَ تُسَافِرُ المَرْأَةُ إلاَّ مَعَ ذِيْ مَحْرَمٍ

(The woman does not travel except with a male relative escort.)[138]

And the narration:

خَيْرُ صُفُوفِ النِّسَاءِ آخِرُهَا وَ شَرُّهَا أَوَّلُهَا

---

[136] Related by at-Tirmidhee and al-Albaanee said it was an authentic narration based on the evidences.
[137] It was traced by Aboo Daawud and al-Arnaoot declared it weak.
[138] Related by al-Bukhaaree and Muslim.

(The best rows for the women are the last and the worst are the first rows.)[139]

And the narration:

صَلاةُ المَرْأَةِ فِي بَيْتِهَا خَيْرٌ مِنْ صَلاتِهَا مَعِي

(The Prayer of a woman in her home is better for her than prayer with me.)[140]

And the narration:

الجُمْعَةُ حَقٌّ وَاجِبٌ عَلَى كُلِّ مُسْلِمٍ فِي جَمَاعَةٍ إلاَّ أرْبَعَة

(The Friday prayer is a right and obligation upon every Muslim in the congregation except for four.)[141]

And he mentioned the woman.

And the narration:

العَقِيْقَةُ عَن الغُلاَم شَاتَان وَ عَن الجَارِيَةِ شَاة

---

[139] Related by Muslim.
[140] Related by Imam Ahmad, Ibn Khuzaimah, and Ibn Hibbaan, both in their *Saheeh*.
[141] Related by Aboo Daawud.

(al-'Aqeeqah[142] is two sheep for a boy and one for a girl.)[143]

And the narration:

عَتْقُ المَرْأتَيْنِ فِي الفَضَلِ يُعَادِل عَتْق الذَّكر

(Freeing two women is equivalent to the freedom of one male.)[144]

In addition to other texts that are countless. Is the woman equal to the man according to the explanation found within the previous narrations or will these texts be despised[145] while it is said, "We live in the 20th century, we should go with the times? It is sufficient enough for us only to ascribe ourselves to Islam!" Yet its commands and prohibitions are rejected just as the callers of these schools of destruction are. May Allah prevent their evil and deliver Islam and the Muslims from them. I ask

---

[142] T.N: This is the sacrifice of two goats or lambs for the birth of a boy or one for the birth of a girl.

[143] Related by Ahmad, and at-Tirmidhee authenticated it.

[144] Related by at-Tirmidhee who authenticated it.

[145] T.N: The literal statement of the Shaykh is, "Or will these texts be thrown upon the edge of the wall" which is figurative. This is why I chose to translate the text as "despised".

Allah to aide His monotheistic religion, He is sufficient for us and the best one to be entrusted. May the peace and blessings of Allah be upon Muhammad, his family, and his companions.

Chapter Sixteen: A Summary concerning what the two *Shaykhs* Ibn Baaz and Ibn 'Uthaymeen wrote concerning the obligation of paying Alms on Jewelry

All praise is for Allah, and peace and blessings be upon the noblest of the messengers, our master Muhammad, and upon his family and companions. To proceed:

His eminence, *ash-Shaykh* 'Abdul-'Azeez bin 'Abdillah bin Baaz has written a brief treatise concerning the obligation of paying alms on jewelry that was published in two editions, the 12ᵗʰ and the 11ᵗʰ from the magazine *Raayat-ul-Islaam* in the first year of its printing in the year 1380 A.H. His eminence included the evidences from the Book and the *Sunnah* concerning the obligation of alms on gold and silver jewelry. Likewise a separate treatise was printed by *ash-Shaykh* Muhammad Saalih al-'Uthaymeen concerning this topic in the year 1382 A.H. He mentions what *ash-Shaykh* Bin Baaz mentioned using the general and specific evidences that prove the obligation of paying alms on jewelry and added the evidences for those who do not deem

---

it was obligatory to do so along with a response to that view.

I want to summarize in this treatise what the two *Shaykhs* wrote in order to enlighten the one who doubts the issue concerning this area of in-depth study based solely on textual facts. The Book and the *Sunnah* point out clear evidence that it is obligatory to pay alms on women's gold and silver jewelry. It doesn't matter if it is meant to be worn or to be rented[146]. It doesn't matter if it is necklaces or bangles or rings or anything else similar that is fashioned from various types of gold and silver. (It doesn't matter) if a certain amount is reached each year, or if it is from one's personal possession of gold or silver or one's merchandise that is sold, whatever is accomplished to reach this amount. This statement is the most correct statement from the people of knowledge concerning this issue based on the evidence of the Book and the *Sunnah* and the statements of the companions. From the evidences of the noble Quran is the statement of Allah Most High:

---

[146] T.N: In some Muslim countries, jewelry is rented out for wedding celebrations, etc.

﴿ ۞ وَٱلَّذِينَ يَكْنِزُونَ ٱلذَّهَبَ وَٱلْفِضَّةَ وَلَا يُنفِقُونَهَا فِى

سَبِيلِ ٱللَّهِ فَبَشِّرْهُم بِعَذَابٍ أَلِيمٍ ۝ يَوْمَ يُحْمَىٰ عَلَيْهَا فِى

نَارِ جَهَنَّمَ فَتُكْوَىٰ بِهَا جِبَاهُهُمْ وَجُنُوبُهُمْ وَظُهُورُهُمْ

هَـٰذَا مَا كَنَزْتُمْ لِأَنفُسِكُمْ فَذُوقُواْ مَا

كُنتُمْ تَكْنِزُونَ ۝ ﴾

{And there are those who bury gold and silver and
spend it not in the Way of Allah: announce unto
them a most grievous penalty. On the Day when
heat will be produced out of that (wealth) in the
fire of Hell, and with it will be branded their
foreheads, their flanks, and their backs, "This is the
(treasure) which ye buried for yourselves: taste ye,
then, the (treasures) ye buried!"}[147]

The meaning of 'burying treasures of gold and silver'
is not paying alms on what is obligatory to pay on
both (gold and silver) in addition to other rights
(concerning the payment of alms). The verse is

---

[147] At-Tawbah: 34-35

_____

broadly applied to all gold and silver commodities
that have not been specified (in name and
description). So whoever alleges that paying alms on
jewelry is only optional based on the generalization
of this verse, then he must produce evidence (for this
view). As for the *Sunnah* then from its evidences are
the following:

One - What has been established in *Saheeh* Muslim
from the Messenger of Allah, peace be upon him,
that he said:

مَا مِنْ صَاحِبِ ذَهَبٍ وَ لاَ فِضَّةٍ لاَ يُؤَدِّي مِنْهَا حَقَّهَا إلاَّ إذَا كَانَ يَوْمُ
القِيَامَةِ صُفِّحَتْ لَهُ صَفَائِحُ مِنْ نَارٍ فَأُحْمِيَ عَلَيْهَا فِي نَارِ جَهَنَّمَ فَيُكْوَى
بِهَا جَنْبُهُ وَ جَبِينُهُ وَ ظَهْرُهُ كُلَّمَا بَرَدَتْ أُعِيدَتْ لَهُ فِي يَوْمٍ كَانَ مِقْدَارُهُ
خَمْسِيْنَ ألفَ سَنَةٍ

(If any owner (*Saahib*) of gold or silver does not pay
what is due on him, on the day of resurrection,
would come, plates of fire would be beaten out for
him; these would then be heated in the fire of hell
and his sides, his forehead and his back would be
cauterized with them. Whenever these cool down, it

---

is repeated during a day the extent of which would be fifty thousand years.)[148]

The one who wears gold and silver is the actual owner (*Saahib*) of the two possessions, there is no evidence to exclude it from this generalization. The due amount on gold and silver is from the greatest and most obligated right of alms. Therefore these two great texts from the Book and the *Sunnah* include all types of gold and silver, as well as other various types of jewelry from the specific evidences, prove the obligation of alms on jewelry.

Two – What has been related by at-Tirmidhee and Aboo Daawud, the wording belonging to 'Amr bin Shu'ayb from his father who narrated from his grandfather that a woman went to the Messenger of Allah, peace be upon him. She had her daughter with her and on her hands were two thick bangles made of gold. He said to her, "Have you given alms on this?" She responded, "No." He said to her:

أَيَسُرُّكِ أَنْ يُسَوِّرَكِ اللَّهُ بِهِمَا سِوَارَيْنِ مِنْ نَارٍ

---

[148] Related by Muslim in the Book of Alms under the chapter "The Sin of one who does not pay the Alms Tax", narrated by Aboo Hurayrah, may Allah be pleased with him.

(Does it please you that Allah will make them two bangles of hellfire, for you on the Day of Judgment?)

The narrator continued, "She then removed them both and tossed them to the Prophet, peace be upon, saying, 'Both are for Allah and His Messenger.'" It is said in *Buloogh-ul-Maraam* that its chain of conveyance is strong.

Three – What was related by Aboo Daawud from 'Abdullah bin Shidaad bin al-Haad that the said, "We entered into the precincts of 'Aaishah's home, may Allah be pleased with her, and she told us that the Messenger of Allah, peace be upon him, came in and saw that she had two thin toe rings in her hands. He asked her, "What is this 'Aaishah?" So she said, "I made them to beautify myself for you Messenger of Allah." He told her, "Did you pay the alms on it?" She said, "No." He said, "It is sufficient enough to protect you from the fire." It was said to Sufyaan how she would pay alms and he said she would combine it with other things (that she paid alms on) and this narration has been authenticated by al-Haakim.

156

Four - And what has been related by Aboo Daawud from Umm Salamah who said, "I was wearing jewelry made of gold so I asked him if what I was wearing was considered hoarded wealth? He responded:

مَا بَلَغَ أَنْ تُؤَدِّي زَكَاتَه فَزَكِّي فَلَيْسَ بِكَنْزٍ

(Whatever reaches the specified amount for you to pay alms then pay it if not then it is not considered hoarded wealth.)

This narration was authenticated by al-Haakim and adh-Dhahabee. Therefore in this narration there are two glorious benefits, the first is that if the allotted amount is not reached then there is no alms to be paid. It is not considered hoarded wealth that has a promised punishment for it. The second benefit is that every possession that is imperative to pay alms on that is not paid, is from the hoarded wealth that a punishment is promised for. And in this is a third benefit and it is the purpose of mentioning which is that it is an evidence for the obligation of paying alms on jewelry.

So if it is stated that maybe this was at a time when wearing jewelry was prohibited as it is alleged by

---

those who do not hold it obligatory to pay alms on jewelry. Then the response is that this is not a sound view since the Prophet, peace be upon him, did not prohibit the wearing of jewelry, rather he declared it permissible but warned against not paying alms. If wearing jewelry was prohibited he would have ordered it to be removed and warned of wearing it.

If it is asked, what is the response to the evidence that has been used by the scholars who do not deem that alms is given for jewelry and it is what has been related by Ibn al-Jawzee with a chain of conveyance that has been looked into and narrated by Aaafiyah bin Ayyub from al-Layth bin Sa'd from Aboo az-Zubayr from Jaabir, may Allah be pleased with him, that the Prophet, peace be upon him, said:

لَيْسَ فِي الحُلِّي زَكَاة

(There is no alms given on jewelry.)

It is relayed by al-Bayhaqee in his book Ma'rifat-us-Sunaan wal-Aathaar.

The response of the scholars to those scholars who held this opinion is based on three views. The first

158

view is that al-Bayhaqee said that the narrative is false
and has no basis, on the contrary it is relayed by
Jaabir as being from his statement and Aafiyyah bin
Ayoob is unknown.

The second view is that if we assumed the reliability
of Aafiyyah as it was conveyed by Ibn Abee Haatim
from Aboo Zur'ah then it does not contradict the
narratives concerning the obligation of paying alms
on jewelry nor can it be compared to them (the
authentic narratives) due to their authenticity and
due to the determination that it is weak.

The third view is that if we assume that the narrative
is comparable and equal to the authentic narratives
and that they contradict this sole narrative then
accepting the authentic narratives is more
comprehensive and whatever is comprehensive is
more befitting to follow. The previous verse and the
four narrations clearly prove that it is obligatory to
pay alms on jewelry made of gold and silver, even if it
was made to be worn or to be rented. As for the
statements of the companions then it has been
related from 'Umar, Ibn Mas'ood, Ibn 'Abbaad,
'Aaishah, and 'Abdullah bin 'Amr bin al-'Aaas, may

Allah be pleased with them all, that they held the
opinion that alms was due on jewelry.

If it is asked what is the response concerning the
evidence used by those who do not hold it obligatory
to pay alms on jewelry transmitted by al-Athram who
said that he heard Ahmad bin Hanbal say, "Five of
the companions were not of the opinion that there
was alms on jewelry, Anas bin Maalik, Jaabir, Ibn
'Umar, 'Aaishah, and Asmaa, may Allah be pleased
with them."

The response is that some of them relayed narratives
that proved the obligation (of paying alms on
jewelry). If we assumed that all of them held to one
statement or that the latter statement from them is
the statement in support of not paying alms on
jewelry then it would oppose the companions who
differed with them. So when there is a dispute
amongst them, then it become obligatory to return
to the Book and the *Sunnah* which both prove that it
is obligatory as was previously stipulated.

If it is asked what is the difference between jewelry
that is owned and clothing that is owned when we

---

mentioned the obligation of alms concerning the first but not the second?

So the answer is that the Legislator differentiated between both whereas He obligated payment of alms on gold and silver without exception, rather there are specific texts concerning this requirement on worn jewelry that is owned as previously mentioned. As for clothing then it holds the same distinction of horses and domestic servants, both of whom the Messenger of Allah, peace be upon him, said:

لَيْسَ عَلَى المُسْلِمِ فِي عَبْدِهِ وَ لاَ فَرَسِهِ صَدَقَة

(There is no alms obligatory on the Muslim for his servant not his horse.)

So if the clothes are to wear then there is no payment of alms due. But if it is to sell them, then payment of alms is due.

If it is asked, is it correct to compare (make *Qiyaas* on) jewelry that is owned and intended to be worn with clothing that is owned and intended to be worn like those who say that it is not obligatory to pay alms on jewelry?

The answer is it is not correct to compare them both due to several views: the first is that this is reasoning by way of comparison in exchange for an authentic text. Every reasoning that is done by comparison (*Qiyaas*) in exchange for an authentic text results in a mistaken comparison. The second view is that alms is not obligatory on clothes to begin with. The need for making *Qiyaas* (reasoning by comparison) is when the ruling concerning jewelry (specifically) is isolated however it is a part of the obligation of alms, whether the jewelry is made to wear or used for any other reason. Just as the ruling on clothing is isolated, there is no alms paid on it, whether it is made to be worn or for any other reason. This does not disprove the obligation of paying alms on jewelry when it is merchandise because the alms at that time is based on its value.

So if (personal) jewelry that is owned (and not for commercial purposes) is different than (personal) clothing that is intended to be worn (and not for commercial purposes), according to these divinely legislated rulings, then how do we obligate or allow combining jewelry with clothing concerning the ruling that the Prophet, peace be upon him, set for voluntary charity?

The response to this is that the issue concerning charity does not establish the obligation of paying alms nor does it negate it. On the contrary, it confirms the command to give charity even if taking from one's everyday necessities as it is said, 'Give in charity even if only a Dirham from your own wealth'. Alms is not obligatory on jewelry until it reaches a certain amount, so the set amount of gold is twenty Dinar and the set amount of silver is two hundred Dirham and the amount of that in the currency of gold is currently eleven Saudi pounds and three-sevenths of a pound.

And the amount of currency in silver is currently fifty six Saudi riyals. So whoever owns the amount of gold and silver previously mentioned or owns cash or merchandise that equals the amount of gold and silver previously mentioned, then it is obligatory for him to pay when a whole year has passed, if it doesn't meet these requirement then there is no alms paid.

Notice: The obligation concerning alms on gold, silver, and cash is a quarter of a tenth meaning 2.5%; likewise the ruling concerning alms on merchandise is based on its value.

We ask Allah the Most High to guide us to the straight path. And may the peace and blessings of Allah be upon our prophet Muhammad and upon his family and all of his companions.

NOTES

NOTES

NOTES

NOTES